And I Thought I'd be a Nun

Georgianne Landy-Kordis

And I Thought I'd be a Nun

Copyright © 2014 Georgianne Landy-Kordis
All rights reserved.

ISBN-13: 978-1499674262
ISBN-10: 1499674260

No part of this publication may be reproduced, stored in a retrieval system or transmitted in any way by any means, electronic, mechanical, photocopy, recording or otherwise without the prior permission of the author except as provided by USA copyright law.

Scripture quotations are from the HOLY BIBLE, NEW INTERNATIONAL VERSION®. Copyright 1973, 1978, 1984 Biblica. Used by permission of Zondervan. All rights reserved.

This book is available in print at most online retailers.

Published by LilyHeart Publishing
Piedmont, Oklahoma

Prepared for publication by:
www.40daypublishing.com
Oklahoma City, Oklahoma

Re-edited by Cindy Jolls Kahland
May, 2018

Cover design by Jonna Feavel

Author photo by Photography by Jonna

Published in the United States of America

'And I thought I'd Be a Nun' is a heart-wrenching, true, family drama about the life, trials, and tribulations of author, Georgianne Landy-Kordis. No book comes closer to exposing the depths of a woman's soul. Forced to deal with extraordinary hardships, death, rejection, abuse, and a struggle to rise above obstacles that would break the spirit of most people, Georgianne shows true strength as she perseveres and overcomes what life has thrown at her. Ms. Landy-Kordis writes in a brazenly honest, fresh style. The chronological events of her life take the reader down a sometimes disturbing yet eye-opening journey that leads to her personal growth and struggle to find self-worth and true love. With the help of friends and a strong conviction that God has a purpose for us all, she has lived a life and written a tale worth reading.

~Susanne L. Lambdin (Author of the Dead Hearts Novel Series)

Dedicated to my husband
Kenneth (Kord)
Whom I love dearly
for giving me the love, support, time and freedom to be creative
and to my gifts from God
Cassandra & Jazzmine & Elijah
Whom I love with all my heart.

Georgianne Landy-Kordis

A NOTE FROM THE AUTHOR

    The wind allows me to enjoy its beautiful, kind singing through the trees to the highly emotional roar of its anger. Some of the most powerful winds blow in and out of Oklahoma. I'd like to think that with every problem or conflict that comes along, the winds could just carry them away. They can't. Problems and conflict often take a long time to solve or be resolved but emotional pain and suffering can take so much longer, and only the strong sustain and survive.

    I've always been able to find a solution to a problem and could usually take care of it quite quickly. A conflict peacefully resolved was my preference but on occasion it got ugly or I simply had to walk away. I was never one to carry a grudge. Why waste my energy on negativity. I think that negativity must take so much more effort and energy than what should come natural, positively and loving. Also I never wanted to carry any guilt or malice in my conscience.

    This book was a long time in the making. I had made notes and started to write it many times. The combination of past paperwork and the reliance of my memory has finally produced 'That Book' I was always going to write. I'm sure I have muddled some of the timelines and have forgotten or not known certain facts. But did I leave things out? Of course, to protect the innocent as they say, and simply because there was just too much needed to keep it flowing and interesting. Did I exaggerate? Didn't have to. I know that others of the human race have faced many similar life situations and emotional stresses. But this is my story to tell as I felt it, as I lived it: good choices, bad choices, strengths and weaknesses. My story.

God has helped me through many, many trials. I praise Him, I thank Him and want to give glory to His name. Christ is my savior and without Him, I am nothing and can never be anything.

Not only did I want to share my experiences, I also wanted to acknowledge, honor and thank God, as well as my friends. God truly blessed me with extremely wonderful friends.

-Georgianne

Psychologist James Hillman - "We are less damaged by the traumas of childhood than by the traumatic way we remember childhood."

CHAPTER ONE

I was born in the simpler innocent time of the 50's. Springtime in Jamestown, NY, the day or time, I never knew. My mother couldn't remember. She could remember the time of her other births but not mine. I doubt she ever bonded with me, but oh how I wanted her to love me. There is a picture I have from my baptism into the Catholic Church. I was nearly two years old they said and the priest was very upset about it. The reason I was not baptized, as most Catholic children within a few days, was never really discussed with me. In this one picture I have, I'm wearing my baptismal dress, and I see how sweetly I am laying my head against my mother just wanting to be loved and protected by her.

I was told that my mother, Grace, suffered from postpartum depression after she gave birth to me, and I was cared for by my Aunt Bea and Uncle Dominic for some time. Bea was my mother's closest sister. My cousin, Patsy who was about six years older than I, thought I was his little sister. "I was sad because you were at our house for quite a while and then they took you away. I thought you were my little sister." He revealed this to me later in life.

My mother was one of twelve children; she was one of the youngest. She described herself as a very ugly child. Red hair, freckles and very skinny. She claims she was picked on by her siblings for being so ugly. Her parents, Clarence and Hazel (Lanning) Logue met when my grandfather worked on the railroad and my grandmother in a restaurant where he frequented. They made a home in Harrisburg, PA, providing for their family on a large farm until they lost it in the great depression. One of Mother's most fond memories was of her sitting watching her father fish. Her most terrifying was when the Susquehanna River flooded in 1936 when she was five, and how she thought, "We were all going to perish." Not the reason she never learned to swim though. She attributed that to her older "crazy" sister, Bessie, who would apparently throw her into the water just to be mean. Nationalities inherited from this side of the family consisted of some French, Irish and a little Shoshoni Indian.

At some point the family moved to Jamestown, because at fourteen my mother was working part time at one of the Landy businesses where she met the man that would be the love of her life and my father. She continued to go to school and graduated with a twelfth grade education. Even though she was an "ugly child," by her teen years she had become quite the beauty.

She knew Donald George Landy was a playboy, but would get butterflies in her tummy and weak-kneed when she would see him. He had his eye on her also and waited until she was old enough to date. She may have played hard to get, especially knowing about his past. She dated a few others and even accepted an engagement ring from one only to break his heart when she gave it back. She told us that my father made sure he would be her one and only.

My father's parents came to America as teens from Naples, Italy. According to my mother, my grandfather changed his last name from Lanni to Landy. My grandmother's last name was Benedetto changed to Baney.

They became Fabio and Margaret Landy. In a letter my grandmother gave me her real name and Fabio's, and names of my great grandparents as well. Their last name was Lanni, from Naples. She only listed the one set as great grandparents which confirmed that Mother was telling the truth when she told us that Margaret and Fabio were first cousins. (I later traced our roots and found that they were cousins because their mother's were sisters.)

Mother also said when they wanted to get married here in America, it was hard to find a Catholic priest that would perform the ceremony. My grandmother told me she came to America first and when she saw my grandfather coming from the train, fresh from Italy, she knew she wanted to be with him. They were pretty young at that time. I think my grandmother said she was sixteen. They had four children, owned the Phoenix Restaurant and Landy Brothers Dry Cleaning business. My grandfather's brother, Fred, owned Landy Furriers; and I also had a second cousin that owned a drug store in Jamestown. My mother also mentioned that there was "royalty" in the family. Something about priests and land and as long as there was a priest in the family, something, something, something. I didn't understand but always wondered what I would have been or am. A Princess? A Duchess? Maybe nothing, I don't know.

My mother always said I was 19 months younger than my brother, Don, but I never questioned it until late in life and actually figured it up only to find that I was only 16 months younger. That would have meant that she got pregnant again only seven months after her first child and perhaps she thought that was too soon. Maybe it looked bad for that to happen, after all she was very conscious of how things looked.

Don and I were very close growing up. It was just he and I until my sister, Teresa, pronounced Teressa, was born eight years later. Mother said it was the French version of the name, Theresa. It may be, I don't know, but you see a pattern here? We didn't question our mother.

My mother was always dressed beautifully then. You know, it was when women wore dresses, heels and hats to match, and the men wore slacks, suits and ties. I thought she was so beautiful and such a lady. She was like a June Cleaver and Jane Wyatt rolled into one. She seemed to be very sweet and caring and I loved her very much and wanted her to love me, but there was a problem.

I remember as a very little girl, my mother was always on to me about one thing or another. For instance, apparently when I was about two or three, I would pick up cigarette butts off the street and put them in my mouth. Now mind you, growing up on a very busy street in Jamestown, NY, and living above the restaurant on one side and the grandparents and my Uncle Jr., aka Fabio Jr., on the other, I'm sure I was only mimicking what I may had seen people do as they came in and out of the restaurant or walking down the street. My mother made me eat a cigarette to break that habit. I remember crying and trying to spit the tobacco out.

**"Oh, that's terrible. I tried smoking once, my mother caught me but I was about twelve.
I got grounded for two weeks. I know that doesn't begin to compare."**

Well I got caught trying to actually smoke, too, when I was nine. Stupid me, I left the butt in the toilet instead of flushing it. I got slapped a few times as she lectured me. She enjoyed yelling and lecturing for several minutes, and sometimes would come back and continue. Sometimes it felt as if it would never end.

I remember my mother telling me what I was thinking or going to do before I was even five. I can still see myself standing in front of her as she, sitting on the bed continually lecturing and shaking me, telling me what I was thinking. I stayed strong in my mind by repeating to myself, "That's not what I was thinking. That's not what I was going to do." I could only shake my head and cry even though I was told I couldn't cry. I was not allowed to show any emotions ever. I'm sure I was a really good little girl. I mean how bad can a child be before the age of five, especially in the fifties? As I grew older she became more sophisticated in her perception of me and began telling me how I would end up. I don't quite remember what words she used, but I can tell you I wasn't going to amount to much.

Thinking about it now, perhaps there was an internal frustration within her and she worked out some of her frustrations on me. Or perhaps as this book called "The Celestine Prophecies" stated, "there were people who tried to take the energy from others." I believe my mother was always trying to take my energy. It's as though I knew this as a child, and growing up because I rebelled, refused to let her take it. I must have known I was going to need all my energy to face the many trials that were about to occur during my lifetime.

My father, on the other hand seemed, to be very easy

going, funny and easily humored. He may have been a little hard on my brother Don, but I am not sure because I only remember one instance when he had gotten stitches in his knee after thinking he could fly because an angel told him so. My father was trying to get him to bend his knee as the doctor had instructed after the stitches were out. I remember my mother getting onto my father about it. My impression then was dad was either hard on him or Mother was too soft and babied him. It may have had something to do with Don being a sickly child when he was born, and Mother said he almost died. Who knows, all I knew at the time was that she didn't love me but my daddy did.

Even though Don was older it was I who learned how to tie my shoes first. It was I who could whistle and blow bubbles from my bubble gum, and it was I who was stronger and wiser. As we grew older, it was I who had the street smarts, the common sense, whereas Don had the book smarts, and it was I who was athletic.

The only chores I recall doing as a child were to make our beds and I had to wash the dishes once in a while. I remember hearing Lloyd Bridges in "Sea Hunt" on the TV and playing with the dishwater. Don wouldn't throw the garbage because it had "germs" so I had to do that also. I swallowed some ice cubes once and the dark "Old English" furniture polish, but I really don't remember. I do remember when a bird somehow got into our bathroom and scared me pretty badly as I sat on the toilet screaming and my hero daddy came in to chase it away.

I ended up with stitches on my ear and missing my Christmas performance one year. Don and I were wrestling on the living room floor too close to our glass coffee table and, well, I can remember Dr. Cameron's red tie that I stared at while he stitched me up.

Stitches to the side of my right eye were added the next year when Don and our cousins ran to the banks of our yard to see where the blaring sirens of fire trucks were going. Factories that lined the streets below us were in view. Because they couldn't see any action, Don decided to run to our apartment to listen to my father's police radio. In my wisdom I knew we wouldn't be able to see anything or I simply wasn't interested, so I stood back and watched them as they all ran to the bank and then they all came running back toward me, Don in the lead and excited as ever. He loved this kind of stuff. I moved out of the way but apparently not enough. He pushed me and I fell, hitting my head on a cement block. Surprised it didn't knock me out. This halted their mad rush to the radio. I was hurt, crying and making my way to the apartment. I stopped and sat on some steps for a minute holding my head. When I moved my hand one of my cousins yelled, "Your eye is bleeding!" Of course this scared me. I cried harder and ran to my mother. Next thing I remember was sitting in the back seat of the car holding a towel to my face and singing in my head of all things, "Happy Days are Here Again" over and over. Perhaps that was a coping mechanism. I know my father was driving, but don't remember if my mother was with me or not. Dr. Cameron stitched me up again. Don really got into trouble for that.

Our life was pretty normal as far as I knew. We were a good Catholic family who spent a lot of time with the Landy family. We ate homemade noodles and meats with marinara sauce, breads and salads with all the family on Sundays in the restaurant. My mother helped with cooking and making the noodles for our consumption as well as patrons of the restaurant, but she never worked as a waitress, my father wouldn't let her she said. Father worked the bar with his dad and brother- in- laws on the weekends.

We ate certain foods on certain nights of the week, such as steaks on Monday, Italian again on Wednesday, fish on Friday of course, and Saturdays was homemade soup, and Mother always had homemade desserts for after dinner. We shopped on Thursdays, all of us: Mother, Father, Don and I. We did everything together. I loved going for Sunday drives and ending up getting an ice cream cone. I remember my dad pointing out an orphanage up on a hill, and with a huge smile on his face saying he was going to put us there. I knew he was kidding.

I got a little pink kitchen set one year for Christmas when I was about five. It was cupboards, buffet, table and chairs and a little tea set with cups. I probably liked it pretty much because I remember Don and I having tea parties. For some reason I put my initials on the top of the cupboards and I got in a lot of trouble from Mother. I mean you would have thought I had desecrated some valuable relic or something. Excuse me, I was just a little kid and I thought it was mine. Didn't care much for having tea parties after that.

Don took piano lessons and even though I expressed wanting to play the violin, that never happened. Instead I was enrolled in ballet and tap dancing lessons and I was a model for a local department store that had fashion shoots and shows. There were plenty of dance recitals, too. I didn't mind tap as much as ballet, and Mother made me practice a lot at home and didn't make it pleasant. She made me hate it even more because she was constantly on me to be perfect.

That's what she wanted from me, to be perfect. She just didn't know I was already pretty perfect, and she didn't have to ride me all the time about everything. She blamed it on my father. She said he told her to make sure I was doing what I should be doing. I think she must have had an internal irritability situation and she had to take it out on somebody. Don was her favorite and then Teresa too as we got older. I was very conscious of these facts. I was her punching bag.

Seems like I was always getting lectured and in the corner for something. My cousin Pat, even as a kid, thought as he revealed many years later, "I never thought you deserved the bad rap you got in life." I didn't think so either and had wondered why for many years. Finally I came to the conclusion that it was my role. Either assigned by God or of my own choosing if there is such a thing as reincarnation, and I had to experience, concur or learn something within this particular life before moving on. Oh, and in this role I made many bad choices.

"Sounds like she was pretty hard on you. She wasn't like that with your siblings?"

Oh, no, not at all. Well my older brother, Don, could do no wrong and Teresa, well it took them eight years to have her so you know she got special treatment. But when our father died she was nineteen months old and our father, because he couldn't work toward the end, had been taking care of her. So she was old enough to realize he was gone. There was this one incident that happened at Christmas two months after his death. It was dinner time and Bea, Dom and Patsy were over. My sister saw our dad's glasses in a glass cabinet in the dining room and she began to scream. She had this habit of tightening her legs when she got mad or upset. She screamed and tightened her legs and cried, and my mother had the hardest time calming her down. Quite an amazing and emotional effect on her. Oh how she must have missed him. Me, I didn't believe he was dead. I thought it was all just a fake deal. I didn't know why my grandparents would do such a thing... pretend he was dead, but they did. It took a long, long time for me to finally believe he was gone. Actually dead.

I remember the last time I saw my dad. My parents were getting ready to go out with my mother's boss. My mother was working at a dry cleaning business because my father was too sick at this time to work. He had rheumatic fever as a child and it left a hole in his heart. My father was so handsome to me. I believe he was a very lovable kind of guy with many friends and someone who appeared to love life probably because he knew his days were numbered. They say he lived about five years longer than expected once he married and settled down. "You're a lot like your father," Mother would often say. "So easy going and easily humored." I do like to be humored and I love to laugh.

My brother and I were getting ready for bed. I jumped into bed and my father came over to me, dressed in his suit and he said, "How do I look?" "Very handsome," I giggled. He kissed me and tucked me in. Sometime in the middle of the night I sensed someone walked by my bed and then I heard someone saying. "Grace, Grace! Donald's in the hospital! Grace!" I heard my mother say something but couldn't make it out. "Grace, he's in the hospital and he's," and the word "dead" came out of their mouth in a cry and stretched out long. My mother screamed, "No" in the same manner and then continued to cry that word, "No" and she came into our bedroom and fell down onto my brother's bed crying. I am sure my brother was freaking out. We were then rushed out of our room, across the hall into our grandparents' apartment. They made us go into our uncle's room, as if we were going to be able to go back to sleep. We could hear our mother screaming, crying and beating on the walls. Don and I came out into the dining room once but we were told to go back to bed. They called a doctor in to give our mother a sedative we found out some time later.

"Oh no. You were how old?"

I was nine, my brother ten. Next thing I remember, we were at my Uncle Louie's and Aunt Gladys's house. It was late October so there was snow on the ground and lots of it that year. I remember building igloos with my cousins, Kathy and Debby. We were only there one day, I think. Then one of my mother's sisters came and got us. Bessie; "the crazy one" according to Mother. She lived on a farm on a hill. My father often referred to it as "the funny farm." I didn't care, I liked it there. I got to wear a pair of my cousin's jeans that day. I was not allowed to wear jeans or pants. I could only wear pedal pushers, shorts or dresses. My mother wanted me to be "a lady" at all times. My uncle Dom would always say, "You kids look like you just came out of a new shoe box." Anyway, so on this "funny farm" of my Aunt Bessie's, we had a few cousins. They lived in an old farmhouse. I remember a hay barn, a pond, some goats and I think they had a small apple orchard.

Even though we were there because our father died, it was like a vacation. Of course, because I didn't believe my father was dead, I kind of enjoyed being there. I didn't know how my brother was dealing with everything at the time, but did ask him years later. He said he pretty much just accepted it and went on.

My sister and Mother were with my Aunt Bea and Uncle Dom. We were all being taken care of by relatives on my mother's side which also made me feel like the Landy's were just punishing us for something, especially when they took us from Uncle Louie's. I believed they didn't like us and that my dad was still alive somewhere.

My mother was not well at all. I think they had to keep her sedated for a few weeks. I remember one evening before my dad's funeral being at my grandparents. Everyone was just sitting around. It was dark and depressing. They may have been talking but I don't remember. I do remember that my brother was trying to say something to our mother but she was non-responsive. She was like in a trance. All of a sudden my Aunt Gladys got up and yelled at my mother, "Can't you hear your son? Can't you answer him?" All of a sudden my aunt Bea stood up and yelled at my aunt Gladys and struck her in the face, and I think my Uncle Louie got into some of the yelling. I had never seen adults yell or hit each other. It scared me considerably.

"What happened after that? Do you remember your dad's funeral?"

Well, I do remember one evening. I think it was the night before the funeral being at my Aunt Bea's house. There again, my mother was just sitting, staring blankly at the floor. Father Angelo Caligiuri was sitting next to her, talking to her. He was a priest that was from the church we attended, and he also held what was called CFO -- bible study meetings at our home and probably some of the other parishioners' homes. I just know he was very handsome and my mother liked him a lot. He became very close to our family, and Mother and I had remained friends with him throughout the years. He had become a monsignor at some point in his career. I know he was a pastor at some churches and I believe an educator until he retired. My mother and I had always kept him in our hearts. Mother had her heart set on him becoming the Pope one day.

So there was one night at the funeral home for the saying of the rosary. There again, my mother sitting there out of it. Still sedated I presume. She said she really didn't remember days prior to the funeral, the funeral and days after. How nice that she could check out. I should have realized and maybe I did soon after that, what a weak woman she was.

I remember not being able to breathe very well. Don and I had never seen a dead person. And here it was. It was supposed to be my father but I still didn't believe it. I still thought it was all a lie and that was just a dummy lying in the coffin. They sure did a good job making it look like my daddy. But that was not my daddy lying there lifeless. This man that loved me so much, this man that I loved dearly, couldn't be gone. The man that played with us, teased us, and took us to parks, hugged us, joked with us, tucked us in at night with a kiss was just hiding out somewhere. This man that looked more like Ward Cleaver of "Leave it to Beaver" but I sensed more of the personality of Jim Anderson of "Father Knows Best." For some reason my grandparents made him leave us.

Why were they taking him away from us? He was bigger than life to me. He was very dashing in his police reserve uniform, and I vaguely remember him in a marching band, although with his bad heart he probably wasn't marching. I know he joined in the singing and festive behavior in the restaurant downstairs on the weekends. Don and I could hear the festive sounds from our bedroom of the people and Dorothy Brooks playing the piano and singing. Every time someone came in the door she would break into playing and singing, "Hail, Hail, the Gang's All Here!" I would sometimes get down onto the floor, press my ear to it so I could hear more clearly. Dorothy played the piano for years at the restaurant.

I was happy to see her one last time when she was in the same nursing home as my grandmother. One year when I went back home to Jamestown to visit relatives, Dorothy was still playing the piano and singing. I got one last performance that brought back the kind of memories that made me wish I could have gone back to that simpler, most innocent time of my life.

My grandfather told my brother to touch my dad's hand that night at the funeral parlor. I was standing next to them at the casket. I looked at my daddy's hands as I had many times before when he napped in the chair and I watched to see if a finger would twitch as they did when he napped. I remember his hands to this day. They were good looking hands. I loved them and still to this day I look at men's hands to find them again or something close. Funny thing to realize as a child -- nice looking hands. I felt sorry for my brother having to touch his hand. I couldn't have and so happy that my grandfather didn't make me. I don't know; maybe a person from the old country of Italy believes that is something you should do. There again I asked my brother Don about touching daddy's hand. He said he didn't want to but just did it because grandpa wanted him to. I don't remember ever talking about daddy after he died. I did read something about Italians from the old country not talking about the dead so as not to bring them back.

    I don't know how any of us mourned. I probably wasn't allowed to. Even animals mourn. With my current husband, we have Shih tzus. Somehow the mama got out of the fence one stormy night and got hit by a car. I thought we should show her to the others, one was her mate and one her pup, Bear, who was about a year and a half. We buried her without showing her to them but I got on the internet when the pup would not come to me, would not eat and seemed so sad. I read where his mourning could last for weeks. It said to hold him, massage him and try to get him to react to normal activities such as the ones he was accustomed to before his mama got killed. It was one of the most pitiful things I have ever witnessed. He moaned a lot. It was kind of like a moan and a sighing together. I held him, massaged his neck, shoulders and back many times during the day. I even went out in the middle of the night a few times to hold him, hum to him and massage him.

    The mama had just had another litter of pups about five weeks before this happened. All had died for some reason except one which we intended to keep. Bear would have nothing to do with his little sister. I think he thought it was her fault his mama was gone. I became her mama. Her daddy didn't care about her, and oh how she wanted to play with her older brother. He shunned her. That was also so very sad to watch. Bears' mourning lasted for almost four weeks. He got better and sometime later even started to accept his baby sister, Babigirl, and became her protector. He was such a mama's boy and he had to grow up and change roles, kind of like me having to grow up and then take on the role of a mother.

The only other thing I remember about the night of my dad's funeral was that I still couldn't breathe and the smell of all the roses was making me feel very sick. My Aunt Bessie took me into the bathroom and told me to take my underpants off. Weird, but I think she thought my skirt was too tight, which it kind of was, but that didn't help much either. I remember what I was wearing. It was a below my knees green skirt, white blouse and a little sleeveless blazer top that matched the skirt. I never really liked it because it always did seem tight around my tummy and the blazer felt like it constricted movement of my arms as well. After wearing it that night, I really hated it.

The next day was the mass before the burial. It was a large church and every pew was full. People were standing along the sides and in the back and even outside the front doors. My daddy was loved by many. Years later I had looked at the memorial book and counted over four hundred signatures. The mass was long and there were so many flowers, especially roses. The smell made me sick. For many, many years, even into adulthood, I couldn't stand the smell of roses. I also could hear my Uncle Louie crying loudly. I don't remember anything after that. I don't know if we went to the cemetery. I don't know how long we stayed at "the funny farm."

The next thing I remember was my mother packing boxes to move from the only home I had known and that my Uncle Eddie had passed away a little bit after my father had.

He was my Aunt Bessie's husband from the "funny farm." I think they had been married many years. They had five children but I think most of them were adopted from other relatives. I remember one of the boys, Ricky, was supposed to be a little wild. He was about my age and my mother told me to stay away from him. I remember playing with him in the basement one time but he never did anything to me, and then again we were alone talking and he never did anything. I thought she just didn't like him. But then his little biological sister, Patty, was taking a bath one evening and they say a lamp fell into the tub and shocked her to death. My mother said Ricky tossed it in there.

"Oh my."

I don't know if she just said that and truly believed it, but he never got in trouble with the law or anything so they either covered it up real well or my mother was wrong. My mother gave my Aunt my little white cotton gloves to put on her hands for her viewing. I don't believe we were taken to her funeral. I don't have that image in my head, thank God. Well, I do in a way because I can imagine. Perhaps Mother thought that would be too traumatic and let us stay home.

"So all these deaths were close?"

Yes. There were three deaths really close to each other: my father, Uncle Eddie and Patty. She was only seven but I still remember her pretty little face with shoulder length blonde, really blonde, hair. Like a little angel.

That was our life then. It was comforting to know that our grandparents, aunts, uncles and cousins on the Landy side all lived next to each other and were involved in each others' lives. It was a good time. It was the foundation of my life and my older brother, Don's life, but all that was about to change forever.

The next thing I remember after my mother packing was when we were in a new place to live. The house was not far from the Landy family, maybe a few miles, but seems like we never got to go there again, or maybe I wasn't allowed to go. My brother may have been able to go visit them but I know I wasn't. I remember my Grandfather Landy came to visit us once but he didn't even get out of the car. It was as if we did something wrong, or they didn't love us anymore. In some strange way it enforced the idea that my father was not dead and that the grandparents were keeping him from us. It never crossed my mind that they could have just been keeping daddy from mommy and not from Don and me. I think in reality from what I had heard many, many years later was that the family kind of just disowned my mother because they thought she was having an affair with her boss when my father was still alive. I would never believe that of my mother to this day. I think he was there immediately after my father's death and she with three children and no money made a decision that she thought was best at the time.

CHAPTER TWO

I don't remember when I actually believed my father was dead. I know that I have only had three dreams of my father in all of my life after his death; two of them soon after he passed away. They were both scary. One even had blood marks, not from his feet but as if he had no feet, and they were both about him trying to reach out to me or hug me or something like that. In my dream I knew he was dead and it wasn't right that he was there, so I was trying to get away from him.

The only other dream I had was many years later. He was wearing a light yellow suit and it was very sunny and my mother, Aunt Bea & Uncle Dom were in the dream also. They were all sitting down in a meadow smiling. It was so peaceful, and everyone was very happy. I have had several dreams of other family members that have passed away, but just those three of my father.

"Probably just too traumatic as a child to have lost your daddy."

Yeah. I knew he loved me; no question that my daddy loved me. The other two people who I always knew truly loved me were my Aunt Bea and Uncle Dom. My mother favored Don & my sister, Teresa, but I had them. My mother would always accuse me of being "Just like your Aunt Bea!" As if that was a bad thing, I would think. Aunt Bea called me "squirt" and it seemed like she was always there for me. I always remember her laughing. If there was anything bad about her, I never knew.

My Uncle Dom used to tease me a lot. "You're going to get coal in your stocking," he would say every Christmas. And I always looked for it too. There was actually some in my stocking one year and I knew he had put it there. I was tickled. I remember he would always sort of scrunch me into the counters with his body and I would just laugh and laugh. He was a big, handsome Italian man who could sleep standing up using one arm to lean against the wall. I heard he learned to do that while in the army.

We would visit Uncle Dom and Aunt Bea all the time. I loved Grandma Landy's marinara sauce, but I also loved theirs; different but equally delicious. I loved playing with my cousin Pat's erector set and his neat little trucks. I was such a sweet little tomboy. The adults got a kick out of me sniffing the butane from my aunt's and uncle's lighters while there. I did love that smell and they let me do it! Ah, life was good before my dad died.

Don and I attended St. Peter & Paul Catholic School in Jamestown. We entered the school building every morning and had to get into line according to our grade and teacher. There was very little talking if any. A bell would ring and we would walk silently to our classroom. There were three floors and twelve grades plus kindergarten. Our coats were hung neatly on hooks outside of the classroom. We entered our room -- again, no talking. Seated ourselves at our own flip top desks where our books, tablets and supplies were to be neatly kept. Before class started we stood and said The Lord's Prayer and The Pledge of Allegiance. First class was always religion. Religion class and English were my favorite classes, and the ones that reflected better grades.

A bell would ring for lunch break. We stood at our desks, filed out row by row. Silently through the halls and into the cafeteria like little well-disciplined soldiers we marched. Once in the cafeteria we could talk. Silently we would say grace before we ate.

I don't remember specific conversations until around sixth and seventh grade. Then it consisted of cute boys, new songs and groups such as Paul Revere and the Raiders, the Beatles, and Herman Hermits.

When we were finished with lunch, we dumped our trash, stacked our trays and supposed to go back to our seats until everyone was finished or until time ran out. There were always a couple of slow eaters. A nun rang a bell. Silence. We stood and pushed our chairs into the table. Ring again. We said a thank you prayer out loud led by one of the nuns. When finished we quietly filed out. Before the school got paved playgrounds we had to go back to our rooms or perhaps we would take a short walk. But after they paved the two areas behind the school, we ran around playing tag or jump rope.

I don't recall playing with any balls at recess. Maybe they thought we'd get too rowdy.

Friday was always Mass, either in the school auditorium with the whole school attending or in the little church on the corner for a class or two to attend. For many years my knees couldn't tan in the area that had knelt on the auditorium floor for such long periods of times.

One time the school had something called "a white elephant sale." I never really knew why it was called that. Basically a garage sale held by nonprofit organizations -- usually schools or churches to raise money for special occasions that may be coming up soon. I have always been curious about this term "white elephant," so I looked it up on Wikipedia.

"A white elephant is an idiom for a valuable but burdensome possession of which its owner cannot dispose and whose cost (particularly cost of upkeep) is out of proportion to its usefulness or worth. The term derives from the story that the kings of Siam (now Thailand) were accustomed to make a present of one of these animals to courtiers who had rendered themselves obnoxious, in order to ruin the recipient by the cost of its maintenance. In modern usage, it is an object, scheme, business venture, facility, etc., considered to be without use or value." Interesting. Anyway that was the first and only time I knew of or attended anything remotely like a garage sale. I thought it was kind of neat. I was looking for white elephants but don't believe I saw one. Don and I probably contributed to the sale but I don't know what we brought. I do know I bought some little something but don't even remember what it was. I feel like it was a small lamp with a hula girl or something from another country. If it was, I am sure my mother got rid of it.

"Why was that? And why didn't you know what a garage sale

was?"

I don't know if there was even such a thing as garage sales then, and even if there were, we were too good for some things I guess. Our mother wanted us to be model everything, perfect in every way according to her. You know, not allowed to get dirty. I was never to be anything but a lady. It was hard, too, being a tomboy. We only ate the best of food also. I didn't know what spam was until after my father died and we had moved. Some neighbor kids ate it, and their family also received some kind of meat and cheese in large square tin cans. I didn't know at the time that it was food from the state for low income families. I tasted the meat once and it tasted like dog food smelled. You know, like the wet juicy dog food in cans. I like the smell, just not sure I like it enough to taste it.

So at the end of recess the bell would ring again, and again we formed silent, neat lines and onto our classrooms we marched. Of course as you can imagine at the end of the day, another bell rang to orderly get our coats and get into lines to walk home, get picked up or take a bus home. The lines were not only throughout the halls, but extended onto the stairs.

One of my most embarrassing moments was on those stairs waiting in line for my bus. It was the last day of seventh grade and everyone had arms full of books, supplies, and bags. Everything from our desks. Well, my arms were full as well. Sister Mary Michael, who didn't particularly care for me, was standing at the top of the stairs. I was about halfway down on another flight of stairs in line waiting. She was a huge and frightening nun. I had just had her as my home room teacher all year. She had caught me writing a story in her class, and I had gotten in trouble for that, as well as talking in class and passing notes.

"You were writing then?"

Well I guess I was trying. But actually after she caught me, made me bring it up to her and she read it out loud and then made me feel like I did something wrong, I didn't write again until my senior year. The story I was writing was about a boy and a girl of course, on a beach. Purely innocent because I didn't know anything about sex or anything in seventh grade, but I still thought I was doing something wrong. Of course, being Catholic everything you do or did made you feel guilty. The note passing was because that year several boys seemed to like me and they were trying to get my attention.

"Well, what happened on those stairs?"

There I was, arms full of books and supplies and hardly a sound in the building. A twelve-inch wooden ruler slipped from my arms. It fell onto the stairs. I bent to pick it up. Sister Mary Michael looked at me. After a few seconds or so, it fell again. She looked. I bent to pick it up. I couldn't believe it but after a few seconds, it fell a third time. Everyone looked at me, and then it seemed as though they all looked up at her as well. As I bent she made some kind of humiliating, threatening comment. Something about some people trying to be a smart-aleck and what kind of punishment could be handed down. I was so embarrassed. As if I would do something like that on purpose. I was so glad to be out of her class.

I say that now because until the seventh grade I had always been teacher's pet and helper. I think she just didn't like me and maybe because she sensed I didn't care for her. She liked my brother, Don. Anyway she was not my ideal picture of how a nun should appear. As I said she was huge, she didn't appear as neat as the others and she didn't have that nice clean starched scent that the other nuns had. A scent that still to this day I will smell out of nowhere and it takes me back. Actually she smelled bad and she thought she could sing. Well I guess she could but it was soprano and everything moved around her face and neck when she sang, as if vibrating. I found out the term is, "she sang with vibrato". Really, she looked like a fat pelican trying to sing. I didn't think she sang very good and had to keep reminding myself that she was a nun and she "was married to Jesus." As an adult now, I realize it's not how well you sing for Jesus, it's just wonderful that you do.

I did enjoy going to school at St. Peter and Paul's though. It was a very important part of my life. A wonderful foundation for discipline, structure, obedience, respect, and perhaps tolerance, but probably most importantly, it contributed to my great faith in God. If you would have asked me then what I wanted to be when I grew up, I would have answered, "A saint." Then as I got older my reply was, "A nun," realizing you had to be dead to be a saint.

In fact, from second grade until my sophomore year, I just knew that I was going to be a nun. When my father died I went as far as to write a letter to the school priest about how I wanted them to take me right then to a convent. I wrote how I wanted to be a nun and that my brother could take care of my mother and little sister. Although I never heard any response, as I grew older, I felt that they understood my desperation and feelings of loss, and they probably kept their eyes on me for a short while.

"I'm sure they did."

When my father died it was like going from heaven to hell. My mother got involved with a very evil man and our lives became hell. Everyone ended up dysfunctional and with addictive behavior.

"Now this was your mother's boss?"

Yes, this was the man my mother worked for when my father became too sick to work anymore. The man that my folks went out with the night of my father's death. His name was Vincent Victor Valentine. He was called Buss. He looked like a middle aged William Shatner but also a little like Jackie Gleason. I heard he had been in the Navy. He had a tattoo on each of his large upper arms. They were in color: American Indian heads. One was a man, the other a woman. He wasn't a tall man. Probably five-foot six, maybe, five-foot seven, but he was stocky on top -- probably from lifting halves of beef or hogs, and the strength it took to slaughter the animals and then all the cutting of the meat. He was a butcher by trade. Yeah, he was pretty buff and a bully.

I remember going with my dad to pick mother up from work one evening. We got out of the car and my dad said, "There's a good ole guy." I looked in the same direction and saw him. I remember his eyes were a bright blue color and glassy like. Unlike anything I had seen before. Didn't look quite right to me with his curly black hair. When telling a friend, many years later about his eyes, this friend who was well versed in biblical quotes and knowledge of the bible itself, told me that eyes such as those are a good indication that the person is possessed. Well, that just confirmed what I had already concluded. After all he was an atheist.

"An atheist? Why did your Catholic mother get involved with an atheist?"

Oh, she was going to "save" him. Well, you can know that never happened. I believe she found herself a widow at about thirty years old with three children. It was a different time then. Women didn't have the resources or job skills they have now. Three children and the Landy's had pretty much disowned her. It was 1961. Buss was there like a vulture.

My mother called my aunt and uncle, Bea & Dom to come over the night Buss tried to molest me, and then beat my mother after she confronted him about the incident. That was the beginning of "hell" for us. For years, I felt like it was my fault and possibly my mother made me feel that way too, time after time. She never said it wasn't, so what is a child supposed to think?

"I wondered what started, what you called hell. I thought maybe something like that might have happened. How old were you?"

I was nine. Still just nine years old. Many years later, while working at the University of Oklahoma, one of the other employees brought their daughter there for the afternoon. She spent some time in my office area just talking and fluttering around. She was nine. I realized then just how little a nine year old girl is. I, too, was a little innocent girl like that once. How could a grown man want to touch a little girl?

So this is how that night went. My mother and brother walked to the store one evening. The store was several blocks away. It was a little store on the corner across the street from a park that we use to play at in Jamestown. It was a nice walk. I remember because my brother and I and friends walked it many times and even rode our bikes there. I don't know if Buss asked my mother to go or

if she just wanted to or who knows. Now that I found out certain things about my mother, maybe she purposely went to the store and left me there just to see if he would do something. Maybe he had said something to her. I don't know, but it's a thought. They took my little sister also in a stroller. Now why would she leave me there alone? Why couldn't I go with them?

So they were gone. I felt a little uneasy. Buss asked me to find him a comb. He was in his underwear only. Tighty whities, which I hate to this day. I looked in the downstairs bathroom first. No comb. He grabbed the area of my tiny breasts from behind. I was nine for God's sake, not much there, but I was starting to develop. I got away from him only to have him follow me and grab me just a few feet from the bathroom which was in front of the basement door. He told me to touch him as he grabbed my hand and tried to put it in his shorts. He said not to tell my mother because she would be jealous. I must have been a bit strong because I didn't and I got away. I ran upstairs to another bathroom thinking that if I find him a comb he would leave me alone. No comb in that bathroom either. He followed me in there and I slipped away from him again. I, as a little nine year old girl, not knowing that I shouldn't go into a bedroom, did. So the last thing I remember is him pushing me down onto the bed and he coming down and my knees going up to keep him from me. To this day I don't know what he did. I don't know if he just got off of me. I don't know if I freaked out, kicking him. Nothing. Even when I went to counseling years later I could never remember any part of that incident. Complete blank as to what happened. I know that he did not penetrate me or they would have surely taken me to the doctor.

"Oh, my God. Terrible. How did you tell your mother what happened?"

Well, the next thing I remember is lying in bed and my mother asking me what was wrong with me. I remember whispering, "Is he asleep?" and well, then, I don't remember, but I guess I told her what happened. And then the next thing I remember is seeing my mother knocked out, lying on their bedroom floor with a stream of blood running down from her temple.

She had confronted him and he hit her or beat her. I don't know to what extent but again, fast forward, because my mind couldn't comprehend what was happening. Next thing I remember is sitting on my Uncle Dom's lap in our kitchen and my mother and Aunt Bea talking. Buss was gone. My mother said when they got home from the store I was crying on the front porch steps. I don't remember that or even how I got into bed.

"Did they do anything to him? Call the police or anything?"

Are you kidding? Different times. Those things were really swept under the rug then I imagine. Too bad because maybe that would have been the end of it. And, oh well, that's not what happened. Sure would have saved many years of the fear, fighting, stress, anxiety, and plotting, planning and attempting murder.

"Murder?"

Instead he was allowed somehow to stay either by my mother's permission, or his bullying, or my mother not knowing how to live and support three children. They never married legally and my mother gave birth to two boys. She had one miscarriage that I know of. Buss owned a meat market and a laundromat and dry cleaning business in Faulkner, a town just outside of Jamestown.

His wife, Shirley, was a plain kind of mousey person. I'm sure he had treated her just as badly over the years. Probably had her beaten down many years before my mother came along. Their son, Jim, was about five years older than me. Strange, I remember them being at our house a few times, and I remember going to a drive-in movie with them once, "The Ten Commandments;" the old one with Charlton Heston.

"I know that one."

Yeah, that movie seems a bit corny now but it was great then. Anyway, I even spent the night with them. My brother, Don, could have been with us too, but I don't really remember. As I say that I do think he was there also. So I guess his wife was babysitting us.

Buss and Shirley had a mobile home on the lake in the canal area, but he was living with us then. They owned a red and white boat and kept it tied alongside the dock only a few feet away from the house. I really liked that. I remember fishing late into the night and getting up before dawn to fish from the tied boat. That was one of the most enjoyable experiences of my life. I also learned how to drive that boat and ski during that summer, almost a year after my father's death.

I loved boats and still do to this day. Even as a little girl at the amusement parks, I didn't really care about riding anything else except the little boats that went round and round in the water. I felt and still feel a peace when near the water. So Buss taught me to drive a boat and I learned how to ski by being left in the middle of the lake with just the belt that goes around your waist to help you float. I was scared to death but after several tries I did manage to get up and became quite a good skier. Don never learned – in fact Don never was the sporty type.

I was though. I was into all the sports in Catholic school: basketball, track, volleyball and softball. I remember always being the captain of basketball and softball and was a pretty fast runner. One of my classmates, though, was just a fraction bit better than me in everything. Patty O'Neil. We were good friends although I was always trying to beat her. The competitiveness was probably good for me. Made me strong and not willing to give up too easily.

Buss accumulated more businesses and I began to learn what it was to work. I automatically became an asset, this working child.

I must say that working at such a young age and working at so many different venues, I did learn a lot. My very first job was at my mother's friend's beauty shop. I was about nine. I got to sweep, clean up and fill bottles. I remember that it didn't last very long. I think I got about fifty cents each Saturday that I went. I liked earning some money although I don't remember what I did with it, probably bought some candy. I also liked getting away from the house. But like I said, it didn't last very long. Soon I was stocking the new grocery store that Buss had built and opened in the small town of Randolph, New York. He first bought a large piece of land and built a laundromat and then built onto the grocery store.

I kind of enjoyed working in the grocery store. My mother worked in the meat department and my Aunt Bea worked in the office. I helped with pricing and stocking, and occasionally bagging. I remember this one woman. She, too, was stocking alongside of me. I remember her because she was very pretty and shapely -- made me think of Marilyn Monroe. She was blonde and I think her name was Marian. I remember some tension because she was working there. As a child you don't really know what is going on, but I think my mother was either jealous of her or Buss was making advances or flirting with her or both. Something like that was going on. I remember feeling scared and also somewhat embarrassed. I don't know if I was embarrassed for her or of them.

There must have been a few times when we went to Randolph that I didn't have to work because I remember Don and I riding our bikes around the school and reservoir at some park. I really enjoyed just being a kid when I was allowed.

At this time, Buss also had the meat market in Faulkner. I worked there also at times. I remember his son – Jim and I rode our bikes from Jamestown to Faulkner and back. It was about four or five miles. Pretty far I thought to be so young and to be riding so far. But it was a different time then -- a safer time. It was the early sixties. Maybe I was allowed to ride that far with Jim because he was older. I don't think Jim and Don cared much for each other, but Jim and I got along fine. He didn't come around much though. Of course when we left New York, I never heard of him or from him again until he was a man and out of the military.

But most of that was not his fault. His father didn't keep in contact with him.

Soon after the Randolph grocery store was built and running, Buss also opened a laundromat in an even smaller town, Cassadaga. This is where I remember I was allowed to collect the money from the machines as well as clean and sweep.

"How old were you then?"

Oh probably around ten, eleven.

"Was his ex-wife and son still around and involved in those businesses as well?"

No, guess they moved on. Hopefully she was relieved to be rid of him. But then, who knows. His son, on the other hand, may have not been happy about losing his father, per se.

Someone had blown the Randolph's laundromat up. Mother and perhaps Buss believed it was Jim. It blew part of the wall out in the grocery store and quite a bit of the laundromat including damaging washers and dryers.

"Why did she think he did it?"

She said Jim was pretty angry with his dad and he had knowledge of explosives. So then began the task of rebuilding and repairing, and guess who had to help with that!

"You."

Yep. I had to go with Buss, not my brother. Me! Always me! I had to help load the damaged washers and dryers onto a trailer, then take them to a barn to rebuild them with needed parts. Then load them up again and deliver them out to people who apparently purchased them. They didn't buy them outright. They bought them by using them -- putting quarters in the machines just as they would if going to the laundromat.

"That would take them quite a while to pay them off seems like."

It didn't matter. Buss was a businessman. He was always

thinking up ways to make money, and as long as money was coming in, he was happy.

I also had to climb onto the new dryers and drill and screw bolts to hold new lattice between the ceiling and the dryers. It looked nice. Thing is, by working a lot at such an early age, I was learning plenty.

"Did you ever really get to play? Or did you just work all the time? What about school?"

Well, when my dad was still alive there was lots of playing with Landy cousins. My Aunt Mary, Uncle Doug and cousin Judy at some time moved off to California, but cousins Kathy, Debby, Greg, Margaret and baby Dennis were still around. I remember playing then. Birthday parties were always celebrated together usually in the restaurant with lots of family and friends. Our life before my dad died was pretty normal and very family oriented. I do remember my cousin, Greg, was a terror though, a real brat. He would chase us and try to fight with us. I remember one time him chasing us with a rake. That might have been the day that I had had enough.

Greg was chasing my brother Don and me. I remember stopping, turning around and somehow I tackled him to the ground. I was sitting on top of him and hitting his head on the ground. My Aunt Windy, his mother, came out onto her second story porch yelling at me, and my mother was yelling at her from our second story apartment over the restaurant. Next my aunt went over to where Mother was and we saw them physically wrestling. It looked as if my mother was trying to push her out the window. It ended quite quickly, and I guess us kids went back to playing.

When we moved away from the Landy's, we moved onto a street that had about 75 children on one block. Of course some were older or younger than us, and we didn't play with all of them. So Don and I had plenty of new kids to play with. We played war a lot. There were apple and acorn trees in the yards which provided our ammunition against our enemies. In the winters we would take all day to build forts and make snowballs. Then just before dusk we would begin to throw them at each other. When we ran out of snowballs we would charge at each other. Our goal then was to destroy each others' forts and repeat the whole process again the next day.

For some reason, Buss bought Don and me brand new Schwinn bicycles. They were shiny blue and white with chrome fenders that wrapped around the thin wheels. We were so proud of our bikes. We kept them cleaned and polished and rode them all over the place. It was the most freedom I had ever had. My mother must have been off working with Buss. Our grandmother, Hazel, my mother's mother, was babysitting us. We were always outside playing and rode far from home, and it was wonderful. We played imaginary city on our street. I always owned a service station and my brother was a cop and owned a radio station. I picked out someone's driveway and the other kids would pull in and ask for gas or check the air in their tires or check their reflectors. I did it all. I liked running the gas station and Don, when not at his radio station, would be giving tickets out to speeders or reckless bikers.

Even when Don and I played in the house with his little hot wheel cars, we would make little city streets. The streets were lined with random books and encyclopedias stacked on one another as buildings. Then for my gas station I would use the little parts such as tires, mufflers etc., that came with model cars. I would have tires piled up in front of my little building as in display for sale and some other parts on the side of my building. There too, Don owned the radio station and was a cop. Goes to show you, sometimes childhood imagination leads to adult occupations. My brother was in radio all his life, and I, at one time, owned and managed a mechanic and body shop with one of my relationships.

Our days were also filled with playing kick ball in the streets in the summer and sledding in the hilly yards in the winter. So even though I did get to play, I still had to grow up fast. And for all the fun I was trying to have, I was still facing many difficulties in keeping my childhood alive.

The fact that my mother allowed me to go places with Buss alone was stressful. She already knew what he had done, but

I had no choice. He would always have a can of beer when driving and expected me to hold it in between swigs. He would give it back to me in a manner of not being able to just hand it to me, but to reach over onto and close to between my legs. He did it clumsily like he didn't know he was touching me. And of course when he reached for it, he would do the same thing. Even though I was holding the can as far away from my legs as possible, yet not making it too obvious what I was doing, he would still reach for the can in the same manner.

There was one time that for some reason I went to the lake with him alone. We took a boat ride and I swam some. When I boarded the boat and began to towel off, he helped me. When we got home (and this might have been the first time my mother gave me the third degree about what went on), at least it is the first time I remember except for the "comb searching night," I did tell her about him drying me off with the towel. There was a fight between them. I remember him taking the window air-conditioning unit out of the window, carrying it through the house and tossing it off the balcony. Those kinds of units were not light then. What a maniac.

"Were all the fights because of his attention toward you?"

I'm not sure, probably not, but I remember Mother getting mad at him at dinner sometimes because he would offer me the sour cream for my baked potato. Oh I wanted it, but there came a time when I wouldn't eat it because of those incidents.

It seems like they went out sometimes and there were terrible fights when they got home. The smell of booze and blood don't mix very well. It's actually one of the most sickening smells there is. I remember more than a few times waking up and going downstairs only to see blood splatters on the walls and floors and that awful smell.

Well, there was this one time we all went to Canada for a few days. The Canadian border was not far from where we lived. Buss made a point to buy me a two-piece swimsuit. It was a really cute one, kind of like a tennis outfit because it had little skirt flaps for the bottoms. I kind of loved it, but of course it caused a fight, so that became a tarnished feeling.

I was surprised we were allowed to continue going to Catholic School since Buss was an atheist. Don and I rode the bus to school when my father was alive, but since we had moved after his death, we then walked to school or rode our bikes. I'd say it was many miles but I think it was less than two. It seemed pretty far though and pretty rough when it snowed. When I was a kid it snowed a lot. I remember snow up to our knees. Sometimes it would start around Halloween and end in April.

There were times when Don and I would go to mass and Buss would fight with my mother about it. Another thing that would make him mad enough to fight was if my mother would make spaghetti sauce. He would often times pour it, including the meatballs, down the sink. Then there were times he would eat it. And he ate like a pig. When he finished his plate, he liked to stick his fork into others' plates and eat what we had. Not sure what that was about because he could have had seconds or thirds for that matter, but he chose to take from us. Maybe it was just about taking from us -- possibly not wanting us to have something that he may have provided, or to show us that he could take it back. Who knows? He was just a pig.

Buss didn't like Italians and would constantly call us Dagos, Wops or Guineas. Not sure, but we believed he had some Italian in him. His mother looked Polish, but we always thought he had some "Dago" in him -- black curly hair, big nose and his name. But many, many years later I met someone who had some relatives with the same last name -- Valentine, and they were from some hills in Kentucky, not Italian. When we were young, we still had to list our nationality when filling out forms for school, etc. I always wrote Irish, Italian. I wonder what he ever put down.

There was this one time when we still lived in N.Y. Buss had purchased an 18 foot Chris Craft boat, inboard/outboard, a nice boat. I remember waking up one morning and there was some kind of restlessness on Mother's part and several phone calls. Apparently Mother, Buss, Aunt Bea and Uncle Dom had been out on the boat the night before. Thank God, Buss thought there was something wrong with the boat. He dropped them all off at some dock, and he was going to try to make it back to where they started from. They all made it home but Buss. I was wishing with all my little heart he had drowned and believe Mother was also. The boat filled up with water and sank. I think it had something to do with the hoses on the engine. Too bad someone who lived on the lake saw him at dawn swimming toward shore and drove a boat out to save his ass.

By this time, Buss had already broken Mother's arm and had beaten her several times. One time her doctor didn't even recognize her. Father Caligiuri and another priest had talked to her many times, but she refused to leave him, or perhaps he wouldn't let her.

One New Year's Eve they had gone out and left me to babysit. I didn't go to bed and I remember trembling. I didn't know if it was because I was cold or if it was the trembling that had started to consume me whenever I felt like something bad was going to happen.

When Mother and Buss arrived home, she sent me to bed. After only a few minutes I heard a huge boom. I ran downstairs only to see my mother peeling what was left of her nylon nightgown from her body and her right hand was black. I had no idea what had happened. She told me she went to light the furnace and it blew up and threw her back into the wall. I was about twelve and didn't know what to do for her. I thought a cold wet towel would help. She said that wouldn't help. I remember her trying to wake Buss, but he was pretty passed out from drinking. He eventually heard her and off to the hospital they went. None of the other kids seemed to have heard the loud boom.

I don't remember how long she was in the hospital. Maybe it was just a few days. I think Grandmother Logue stayed with us. When Mother told me they bathed her in Tide Detergent Soap, I thought how that must have hurt, but just the opposite she said. The worst burn was to her hand. She healed very well and only had one tiny scar on her tummy. Freckles never grew back in the area of the burnt hand, but no scarring.

One other night Mother and Buss came home from work and I saw her finger wrapped up in gauze. I asked her what happened and she replied as she walked by, "I cut my finger off." It not only made me sick to my stomach, but it scared me too. She hadn't cut it off. I found out later she had cut a large slice from her index finger on the meat slicer. They grafted a piece of her skin from her arm to repair the finger. Mother had no fear and apparently no clue or sensitivity to a child's fears.

My littlest brother, Fred, was probably about two when my mother called Buss telling him that she couldn't find him. She was acting crazy about it. I know that I found him behind the couch asleep and she put her finger to her lips for me not to say anything. I assume by now and by her actions, I knew my mother was one big dramatic actress. For what reasons, I had no clue, but I was just so afraid of her and Buss and the situations that would cause a fight. All I could do as a child was go along with my mother. I don't know what her deal was that day. I am sure she had a crazy reason, but I didn't know what it was. I think he rushed home to help look for him, but in the end she said she found him. That is all I remember of that incident. Just drama -- she loved the drama.

Fred. My mother had legally named him Vincent Allen Valentine. When he came home, Buss started calling him, Freddie. When he began to crawl, Buss would say, "Come here, Freddie. Here Freddie, here Freddie," like calling a dog. So he then became Fredrick Vincent Valentine legally. Fred was never baptized into the Catholic Church, but Mark, who was a few years older, was.

So there were many fights and lots of drama all the time. I just don't know how often the fights stemmed from his attentions on me, but they did continue as did the drama my mother seemed to create. These things went on week after week, month after month and year after year.

CHAPTER THREE

I considered going to a convent again when I was in the seventh grade. There was an assembly for the girls. Several nuns and novices came from Buffalo to talk to us and try to recruit us into the sisterhood. I was so moved and anxious. There was a novice there who had been our babysitter for a short time when our dad was still alive. I remembered her. I thought seeing her was like looking at an angel. We talked. How special she seemed to me. How peaceful and sweet. I wanted to experience that peacefulness, that sense of holiness.

I remember going home that evening and telling my mother about seeing our old babysitter and that she was now a nun. I don't remember our conversation about it or if we even talked about it much further. I know my mother expected Don to become a priest, but I doubt she had any expectations or any good ones of me or for me since I have no recollection of any positive, heartwarming or encouraging conversations with my mother about me or my future -- ever.

I went to my room and began to write this novice a letter. Again, it was about how I felt I was ready to serve God. I went on to write how unhappy I was at home. I never got an answer from her. I know that their superiors read the novices' letters first, so I don't know if she even saw my letter. Oh well, the feeling and thoughts of becoming a nun passed with time. By tenth grade I had been through enough of life's troubles and trials I had started becoming rebellious, hardened and hateful in my thoughts. Also I had always liked boys, even as young as when in kindergarten. I thought they were so cute. I didn't know what to do with them, but I still liked them.

And it seemed like seventh grade brought me many would be suitors if I would have been allowed to socialize with boys. I remember a boy who liked to carry my books for me as I walked home, and there were two boys who liked me at the same time.

One was an eighth grader. His name was something like Bentley and he looked like a Bentley. He was tall, very thin and had perfect posture. He would have been called a nerd if that word was widely used then. He's probably a doctor or millionaire now. The other boy had lots of sandy blonde hair and quiet. I thought he was very cute even though he reminded me somewhat of Ed Sullivan. Bentley was quite determined to have me for his girlfriend. He would come into my class and give me notes and try to talk to me, but I would ignore him. I was very embarrassed, too, that he was pursuing me because he was so nerdy. He even called my mother once and asked her if he could treat me to dinner at a chicken place. To my surprise she said yes. I never did go on that date for some reason, but I remember talking to him at a baseball game that I had gone to with our friend, Bessie Kay.

Bessie Kay, as long as I can remember, was always at our house. She was a little girl who said she loved my dad, and would sit on the steps waiting for him to come home. She lived a couple of doors down from my grandparents' restaurant. She must have been about seven when she met my mother. She remembers that apparently my father asked mother to buy a gift for this little girl. When Mom met her and presented her with a little baby doll, she apologetically said she thought that Bessie Kay was a very little girl. Bessie Kay said she didn't mind and she treasured the doll for many, many years. She and Mother hit it off, so she became like part of our family. After Don and I were born and older, she babysat us. As we grew even older, she was still like a member of our family. We kids spent time with her even when she was married, and in turn babysat her son a few times.

I know that Bentley knew that this other boy liked me, too. On one of those last days of school there was a picnic with food and games. Both of the boys were trying to keep my attention, but I was expected to be doing the races that day. While I was running and trying to win at competitive sports, the two boys had gotten into a little scuffle over me. In the end I lost both suitors. That was all right with me though, because I had a little neighborhood friend that I played with and he was the cutest of all. What's really funny is that there was this one boy that I liked from kindergarten till we left New York. His name was James Landringin. He had the cutest face, but he never liked me – not even a little bit.

"When did the family leave New York? And how did that go? How did you feel about it?"

Don and I never saw it coming. The other three children were too young to know what was going on or to even care. I had gone to the first day of my eighth grade and Don to his tenth grade. When we came home, there was a U-Haul trailer in the garage. We were told we were leaving and couldn't tell anyone goodbye.

I remember looking out the car window and seeing some of our friends on their bikes looking at us as we passed by. I meekly waved at them.

We drove to the lake where Buss had the boat out of the water at some marina. We unloaded the U-Haul of its contents into the boat. The contents mainly consisted of washer and dryer motors and some luggage full of clothes. I don't remember what else there may have been, except for a suitcase containing eighty five thousand dollars cash.

I do know there were no personal items, not our bikes or the skates that belonged to my mother and dad that Don and I use to put on and skate in our attic. Everything was just left behind. Some things went to my Aunt Bea's, and I think Buss gave the bikes to the kids of the family that was going to buy our house.

"Did you feel like you were being kidnapped?"

I don't believe so because we were with our mother. I guess as a child you have some amount of trust if you are with your parents or parent. I actually was a little excited. There was no definite destination so I was hoping for California. Then I could make movies one day. Plus, we had been to California when my dad was still alive, and I absolutely loved it. I loved the weather, the swimming and just the great feeling of being more alive out there. I heard it was the ions from the ocean that gave you more energy. I was sad when we went back to New York, but my father was just as sick out there as he was at home. And, the reason for going out there was to see if he could feel better.

"What was the reason the family was leaving New York now?"

Buss. He didn't want to pay child support or alimony anymore. This is what I heard, and it was also the reason we couldn't tell anyone we were leaving or contact anyone ever again -- not our family or friends. No one. At some point when we were settled, my mother was allowed to tell her sister, Bea, of our whereabouts, but she too couldn't tell anyone where we were.

My aunt told me once that my best friend, Karen Lumia, would ask her about me, but all she told her was that I was okay so she wouldn't worry. Karen and I used to be best buddies in grade school. She was considerably short and a nervous little girl. Sometimes she would stand on my feet facing forward and I would walk carrying her down the hall like that until a nun would get on to us. I used to like going to her home to play. I remember she had a slobbering boxer and an ugly old man finger puppet that I named Burfer. I continually made her laugh by the silly voice and antics he would perform.

I really hated to lose my friends back there. That was eight years of friendship gone, never to be revived again. I remember Donna Armeli, Patty, Karen, a Rita, Collett and faces of boys but not their names. My girlfriends use to call me Lannie Long Legs, I think because of my athletic abilities and I loved it. Except for my mother always on my ass about one thing or another, I loved my life before my dad died.

Losing the Landy family though was the toughest and Aunt Bea, Uncle Dom and Patsy -- oh and Bessie Kay. They were part of our whole life then and it was gone in an instant.

I can't imagine. So you were hoping for California. Did anyone have a clue as to where he was taking the family?

No, no idea. We just drove south and then west on route

66. I kept my brother, Mark and Teresa occupied by acting out scenes with my hands while mother tended to Fred. Teresa was about six, Mark four and Fred one. I made my fingers appear like tiny dinosaurs that walked around on our legs and arms, and made them appear to be eating and fighting with each other. Don probably just sat there looking out the window. I don't remember playing any kind of games such as counting cars or whatever other games most children or families play on long trips.

Mark got very sick on the trip. I think he had hit his head before we left New York and maybe he had a concussion. I remember one night we stayed at a motel and they took him to a hospital to get checked out. Next day though we were off again. You would have thought his head was used to getting hit. When he was still in his crib he would get down on all fours and bang his head into the crib to either move it around the room or perhaps it was a useful mechanism for relaxation. Even though that sounds like strange behavior, we thought it was quite normal for him. In our defense the crib's head and foot boards were made of thin material.

We never had a problem with the car or the boat until we passed through Vinita, Oklahoma. We drove under this big restaurant that spanned across the highway. It was called "The Glass House" then. Odd because after we drove under it still heading west, we encountered a flat tire on the boat trailer.

Buss pulled over and took the tire off and unhitched the trailer. He left Don and I there as the rest of the family went back to Vinita to get the tire repaired.

I knew we were in Oklahoma, but the only thing I knew about the state was that it was inhabited by cowboys and Indians. It was late August 1966. It was hot and windy. Don and I sat on the edge of the highway facing some wheat fields. I felt like it was sunnier than in New York and definitely hotter. I was looking for the Indians though because I was afraid there might be some that would come get us.

When the tire was put back on the boat trailer we drove back into that town of Vinita and spent the night. It was very hot and humid in the evening and we were allowed to get an ice cream cone in a "Dairy Delight" or something like that. There were some older, boisterous teens laughing and having fun -- the kind of fun and freedom I hoped to experience one day.

    The next morning we continued west. I was still hoping for California. No one was saying anything different so my hopes weren't shattered yet. We kept getting flats on the boat trailer off and on into the middle of Arizona. That's when Buss decided to go back to that little town in Oklahoma. I was unaware that he had checked it out and talked to some business people while we spent the night there. He must have thought about it for two states and decided that is where he wanted to start a new life, build a meat market and live right next to it in a mobile home. My hopes shattered.

CHAPTER FOUR

Public school in Vinita, Oklahoma, was such a drastic change. I was not use to changing classes, crowded halls and noise. I had only mere minutes to unlock a combination lock, grab my books and be seated in my next class. I had never been around a black person. Although I was not prejudice, I did feel uncomfortable. Some of the girls seemed tough. In ninth grade there was one black girl in particular who absolutely hated me. She had a group of friends. She was in my Home Economics class, and very hateful and rude to me in class and in the halls. I tried to ignore her. I couldn't understand what her problem was. I imagined myself at any time getting jumped by her and her friends. I prepared myself daily. I thought, "I'll fight with all my might. I'll take everything out on them -- all my hurt, my frustration, my hate, absolutely everything and we'll see who's left standing." I even carried a little fake metal gun that looked real. I know you couldn't do that now, but that's just how threatened I felt. I also know that carrying a fake gun was stupid, but I was young and thought as a youngster. Nothing happened that year, no fights at least. I guess she kind of got over it by the next year. I don't remember seeing much of her after the ninth grade. I think sometime within those next two years she got pregnant. She may have left for a while and then came back.

"It sounds like you had a hard time right off the bat in public school."

Well, at first it seemed that I was about two years ahead of them scholastically. I remember one time when answering questions in class, a girl sitting a couple of seats back called me a smart ass. So, what I thought was a good thing, apparently made me stand out, as well as a smart ass, and she didn't like it so I quit doing it. I had enough trouble trying to fit in. And I so wanted to fit in, somewhere, anywhere as any kid would. The Okies thought I talked too fast, walked too fast and talked funny. I thought they talked too slow, walked too slow and talked funny. We had a hard time understanding each other. I couldn't distinguish between their, pin, pan or pen. They all sounded like pin. Were they saying, him or hem? Tire or tired? I didn't know what a 'battry' was. Thank goodness for context. A bag was a sack which sounded tacky to me. Ground beef was hamburger meat and franks were weenies. Cube steaks were chicken fries to them. I mean what was a chicken fry and what does it have to do with a square piece of tenderized beef? I didn't know what okra was, never had beans and cornbread or white gravy.

I am sure my brother and mother faced the same problems. In fact one time a woman wanted someone else to wait on her in the market. She said my mother was a foreigner and she couldn't understand a word she was saying.

"Well it must have gotten better at some point."

Eventually my classmates and new friends had gotten used to me and I to them. Public school also introduced me to the little cliquish groups. We didn't have that in Catholic school.

The smart kids approached me, wanting me to join their group: Marsha, Nancy, Terry and Karen. Actually, Marsha was my first friend in Vinita. She lived close to where we lived before the meat market was built on the other side of town, and we walked to school together and spent time together on the weekends just messing around outside. Marsha probably didn't know how much that meant to me just having a new friend. I hung around these girls for a while but as I observed each group, I soon realized that I was not as intelligent as these kids. Besides that, the popular kids were the ones having the most fun. I wanted to be with them. It wasn't as though I shouldn't have been, I qualified. Not only did I come from a wealthy, upstanding family back home in New York, but here in Vinita we had our own business, a new Cadillac every year, a truck, a boat and later our own five passenger plane.

The plane was basically used for pleasure trips.

Occasionally we would fly to Oklahoma City just for breakfast. One time Buss was in the wrong place in the air after take-off. I could see from the windows jets at 7:00 and another at about 5:00 coming toward us. I could hear the traffic controllers trying to salvage what could have been a huge catastrophe. Not sure if Buss was drinking that early in the day, but most times he flew while drinking beer. Another time we flew to Six Flags in Texas for the day. After we took off for home and well into the air, I noticed that my mother hadn't latched her door. The latch was above her head. She was holding Fred and looked back at me and realized that I knew. She put her finger to her lips for me to be quiet. I can't describe the stress that I experienced as I tried to calculate how that door would or wouldn't come open and suck mother and Fred out and possibly the rest of us as we began to descend and crash in a fiery explosion. I knew I had to keep my mouth shut because I could also imagine Buss pushing mother out or becoming a raving maniac about Mother forgetting to latch it and having the same end result of a fiery end to our lives.

"Your mother was very brave, wasn't she?"

Sorry to say, not afraid of anything. I guess she was hoping for the best that day and by God's hand we landed safely and Buss never knew about the unlatched door.

I think Don was immediately accepted into the popular group. I felt like I had to work at being accepted -- not really sure why. Perhaps I wasn't cute or pretty. After all, I wasn't allowed to wear makeup for a long time or maybe because I was quiet and shy and probably odd to them. Well, I was dealing with a lot of things. I had to work and take care of my siblings all the time, not to mention the alcoholism, fights and abuse to contend with.

Although the popular kids were the ones I mostly associated with, I always remained warm and friendly with all of my classmates. Even at earlier school reunions I managed to visit with pretty much everyone while most others stuck to their old familiar groups. This was a good thing because it was I who managed to get some former classmates to an all-school reunion a few years before our fortieth. My friend, Connie from Cape Cod, even managed to get to Oklahoma for that. Then I used my organizational and social abilities to head the efforts of our fortieth reunion.

In eighth grade science class one day, a girl a couple of desks behind me and to the right out of nowhere called me a homo. It was Connie. "I bet you don't even know what that is?" I didn't but the girl sitting right next to me did and said, "Of course she does." The girl defending me was one of those wild girls. She smoked and was in a girl rock band, but for some reason she was nice to me. Connie, who is now one of my best friends and possibly my "soul mate friend" as my best friend Vinnie calls her, says she didn't even know what it meant at the time. She admits to getting into trouble many times because of her mouth. We laugh now whenever I bring it up.

Connie and I didn't really run around in high school together. I had to work in the market all the time. She spent her spare time at the Country Club and she belonged to the other girls club, JUGS, "Just Us Girls." I belonged to "Sophisticated Skirts." My club was the kinder, gentler girls. I heard JUGS were a bit wild. Heard they drank beer and smoked. I don't know if they did or not. Some were girls I hung around with and I still didn't know. Connie and I did go on a double date once. There was one of those auctions where they auctioned off the senior football boys. We had outbid the other girls on a couple of guys. Connie and I probably had more money than the others or perhaps we wanted it more. I bid on the only boy I thought my mother would actually let me go out with. Steve was a friend of my brother's and an altar boy at the church we attended.

I felt a little bad when I outbid this one girl, Jan, who really liked Steve. I wrote her an apologizing little letter. Years later she told me she had saved it -- had it clipped to her bulletin board. I always did have a way when it came to writing letters. I wonder if she still has it.

I wrote a letter to a car dealership that sold me a car at age twenty three. It needed several hundred dollars worth of repair. It was a trade-in and I suspected that they never even looked at it before selling it to me. I had a mechanic friend look at it after I had experienced some kind of engine problem. He estimated it needing about fourteen hundred dollars worth of repair. The clincher was when I noticed the spare tire had been cut three quarters around it. I was so mad. I wrote to the owner and demanded that he call me within ten days or the car would be driven through his front showroom window. I really had some balls, didn't I?

He called me on the tenth day and asked me what I wanted him to do. I told him I wanted it fixed. The little red and white '73 Pinto was repaired and a new spare tire given. I was very satisfied and the car lasted me, a single working mom, a very long time.

So Connie and I went to the bonfire and out to the local truck stop for dinner with my date, Steve and hers, "stone face" Wayne. I guess we went to the truck stop because it was very late and well, there weren't many places to eat in Vinita let alone a place open late at night. It was probably a great night for me although I was worried as to what the repercussions would be once I got home. Like the night I went to a pageant at the high school. It was for Miss Grand Lake. My mother dropped me off and I was to get a ride home from a friend. The whole time I was there I was sick with anxiety. I just knew something bad was going to happen.

I got home safely the night of the pageant, but there had been trouble at the house earlier with some friends of theirs. They had all been drinking and I think these friends had gotten into a fight but had gone home. So I felt a bit better thinking that's why I was feeling sick and panicky so I went to bed.

At some time later my mother came into my room and took me to their bedroom. She probably was pulling me in there. As soon as we got to the door and close enough to the bed, she in some way tried to rip my pajama top off and throw me onto the bed at the same time. The buttons broke off and I clutched my top to cover myself. She yelled something like, "There, you want her, there!" Buss was sitting up in bed. I landed somehow just at the foot of the bed, scooted to the end and sat there for a moment holding my top together and probably crying or more likely holding it in. They were yelling at each other and after a few moments, I left the room as they continued to fight. Mother brought it up once when I was much older and revealed that Buss had said to her that night, "Why don't you let me put it in her and shoot it in you?" Apparently that wasn't the only time he had thought of or had said something such as this.

"Terrible thing to do to a child."

I was a teenager then.

"I know, but still a child. There again, his attention towards you."

Yes, but there were other instances where maybe it wasn't because of me. I know that Buss used to accuse my mother of cheating. I remember him mentioning an electrician, insurance agent, our employee, Norman, and a man who owned a pest control business. So these men or others could have been brought up to provoke a fight at any given time.

Occasionally our horses escaped from the field in the middle of the night and would run down to the sale barn which was less than a quarter of a mile away. Buss either didn't care to go round them up or was probably passed out. I remember one night for some reason this man who owed a pest control business was helping Mother and me round them up and get them back to our place. Buss accused her of letting the horses out and calling him just to meet up with him. In actuality he just happened to see what was going on and pulled over to help. Hell, Buss wouldn't hardly let Mother even go to town and she worked side by side with him for up to fourteen to sixteen hours a day, six days a week. How and when would she have time to have an affair?

The six days didn't mean she got to rest much on Sunday. Well, maybe she did some but I doubt it. I know that I didn't get to rest. I had to do the extra cleaning in the market on Sundays. The meat cases had these plastic green leaf-like dividers that had to be hand washed. The cases also had to be washed down with soap and water. This was a bit of a nasty job. Meat was stuck between the green leafs, and I had to really work at them to get them clean. The cases smelled of the blood that had dripped down into them. It was a messy, wet job but very rewarding when done.

Sawdust was still allowed to be used on the floors to collect meat that would fall to keep people from falling and easier clean up. During the week we could rake it and scoop the meat up, but on Sunday I had to sweep, mop and put new sawdust down as well -- equally rewarding. I also had to unload alone the pigs or cattle in the pens for slaughter should a customer bring some in on Sunday. As afraid as I was, especially with the bulls, I would have done anything not to have disturbed Buss. It was dangerous sometimes, especially when there was an unruly bull to contend with. Thankfully, I never got hurt.

I know that we children would try to go to church, but that usually ended up with them fighting about it afterwards so we didn't always go. Don and I were fortunate. We both got a good solid foundation before my father died having gone to Catholic school, church and catechism classes. Unfortunately, my younger brothers and sister did not have the same opportunities. Surprisingly they had good hearts, were good kids and grew up to be good people, but with addictive behavioral problems.

My brothers were pretty wild though -- more ornery than anything I guess you would say. When Mark was about six and Fred four, Buss bought them each a little Honda cycle. These were miniature bikes decked out just like an adult bike. The little hellions rode them like pros. They had no fear. One time when they were a bit older and probably had other cycles by then, they rode to town. A police car was parked in an alleyway. For some reason they decided to let the air out of the tires. They also had been chased by the highway patrol one time and they cut into fields and got away. I never saw them get into trouble for these things. I was in school, but I heard about them because Buss got a big kick out of their escapades. Buss either talked their way out of the trouble or paid a fine. Money talks.

And although again I was in school and never witnessed it, I did hear that my little brothers harassed the help in the market. A time or two they had gotten under the meat cutting tables and would try to hot shot the employees as they walked by. Here again, Buss thought it was funny. I'm sure mother stopped it. Also Mark and Fred would go into the cattle pens and try to ride the cattle -- even the pigs, while the animals were penned up. They were little hellions, that's for sure.

One night, and I don't know why, but my mother was going to do something to Buss, and I knew it. I was trying to keep my brothers and sister occupied outside as I knew that something bad was about to happen. And like I said, I don't know what provoked such action, perhaps not because of me, but possibly just a buildup of pure, unadulterated hate.

Buss was taking a bath and well, my mother took a baseball bat into the bathroom to bash his head in perhaps. Well that didn't work. I remember after he came out of the house, I ran in to check on Mother and saw that he had broken her nose. I have never seen a person with a broken nose. Not only was it broken, but he had hit her with such force that it had split her forehead open and her nose was in a position of that of a pig's snout.

When I saw that, I was sick to my stomach and enraged. I wanted to kill him. I grabbed the bat; he was outside, still in the front yard. I remember swinging that bat as fast and hard as I could, trying to hit his head. He stood there and took several hits to his shoulders. He had very broad shoulders and hardly a neck. I swung that bat several times, but just couldn't hit his head. God, how I wanted to hit his face. God, how I wanted to kill him.

"Where were the other kids while this was going on? Where was your mother?"

You know I don't remember where the little brothers and sister were during those moments. My mother was probably in the bathroom, washing blood from her face or something. My brother, Don, just happened to pull up with his friends. All I remember after that is Don trying to beat Buss up and his friends were holding him back. Buss ran into the market. My brother found a couple of rocks and threw them into the two large windows of the market shattering them.

I don't remember anything after that until I saw my

mother in a bed at Ruby and Del's house. They were an older couple that worked for us. Ruby was our housekeeper and her husband sometimes drove us to school. They were originally from Mississippi. Ruby's hair was white. She told us something about a lightning strike and her hair turned white at a young age. Del was a very poor and slow driver, and I hated having to ride with him. One of Ruby's favorite phrases was, "It's fixin' to pour down rain." I don't know when they left our employment, but for all the years my mother and Fred would use that phrase if it looked like rain, and we all remembered them fondly.

I don't know how mother got to the hospital for her broken nose or how many days passed till I saw her at Ruby's. I think I was staying there also and probably my little brothers and sister, because where else would we be? I couldn't stay home because Buss would have probably tried to rape me or at least sexually harass me.

I don't know how long we stayed there or how long it took her to heal. But I do know we were back home with things as usual, as always, soon after.

Don didn't live at home so it was odd that he just happened to show up at that moment when he did. Buss never liked Don because he had no use for him as he did me. Don got lucky and moved out probably about a year after we moved to Vinita. He lived with friends. How lucky he was to have escaped.

There was another time that Buss and mom were fighting, arguing at first in the kitchen. Again, I was trying to keep my little siblings occupied outside. Well, Teresa, probably about eight, kept running up to the house and looking in the window. I remember her running back to me crying and screaming. Then she would run up to the house again, look in the window and come running back to me screaming for me to do something. I couldn't take anymore.

I ran into the market and got a knife. I ran to the house and opened the door, hiding the knife by my side. Something was said by one of them, and then he said something to me and I told him to shut up. He told me to shut up. Then I said, "You shut up!" He told me again to shut up and I came back with, "You shut up!" and pulled that knife from my side in a threatening gesture at him. My mother saw the knife, gave me one nod and then she picked up a kitchen chair and hit him dead center in the stomach with it. He ran out the other door, she followed and I also went toward him. Somehow my mother got him in a headlock as I approached. She looked at me as if she expected me to stab him in the face. I have thought about that over the years and think, "How in the hell did she think I could stab him in the face -- come on!"

After a lot of struggling, he got loose but fell. He scrambled to his feet, but fell over a little curb that was there. Again, got to his feet, all the time we were following him. He fell over a small shrub, got up only to run a few feet and fell into the picnic table, then fell over the bench. Finally he got enough footing to run without falling and ran down to the sale barn, away from us. Now maybe his falling had something to do with only having socks on his feet -- no shoes, but I like to think he was terrified of me coming at him with a knife, perhaps knowing I was going to try to kill him, again!

"Oh my. I'm sure he was."

This was the first time ever in all the years that he left the house -- not us. Mother and all of us children walked that old highway many times to a motel for the night. He apparently had called the highway patrol, but they must have advised him to leave that night. I was sitting on the couch when he came back to the house with the police outside waiting for him to leave. He was putting some clothes into something like a backpack at the kitchen counter looking at me. "You think you're a pretty big girl now, don't you?" I remember him saying. I didn't reply. I was watching something on TV that I wanted to watch earlier. Again, I don't remember seeing Mom or the kids. I just remember at that moment I was happy that he was leaving, and I was watching something that I really wanted to see.

That might sound selfish but my life was not my own. It was theirs -- all of them. I didn't have my own life. It was full of them, the ugliness, the responsibility, the work, the "Do as I say! Don't think, don't feel, work, take care of the kids, and let me abuse you, use you for my punching bag and whatever I do, you better back me up." That's what my mother expected of me. It was a life of lies and repairs, pain, abuse and dysfunction. But that night, I felt a little victory, and it felt good. And yes, I might have killed for that victory. I just might have killed for that victory, but fortunately I didn't have to that night.

I imagine that some of the times that I don't recall where the kids were could be because of the traumatic situations, but also they would climb out of the windows, run to the field and hide. I do remember having to go find them several times when the fighting was over. I remember a couple of times they even crossed the highway to get away. They weren't babies but considerably young. They were eight, ten and thirteen years younger than me so you can do the math.

CHAPTER FIVE

My mother put a down payment on another house in Vinita without Buss knowing. It was our hidey house for several months before he found out. I stayed there during my senior year.

"I've never heard of a hidey house. How did she keep it a secret?"

Buss would put hundreds, if not thousands of dollars, in the freezer at night. It was money we made during the day in the meat market. He would wrap the money up like it was a piece of meat, take it to the house and put it in the freezer.

My mother devised a plan. One day she told me to call her on my lunch hour at school. "And don't say anything, just listen. Call me at eleven thirty and when I answer, do not say anything, just listen and when I say hold on, hang up."

I was scared when I went into the principal's office to make the call because whatever she had up her sleeve I knew it had to be something bad. I called the market. She answered. "Valentine's. I'm sorry, what? I'm sorry. Wait, can you hold just a minute, I'll get my husband. Hello, hello! Hold on." I hung up.

I didn't know why she wanted me to call until I got home that day. The call was supposed to have been an irate customer -- a man who was unhappy with the job we did on his custom order. That is when a customer brought their own stock in to be butchered and cut up, packaged and frozen.

She led everyone, including the police, to believe that this man called pissed and threatening, and then somehow he went into our house, ransacked it, found the four thousand dollars that was wrapped like meat in the freezer, and supposedly stole our movie camera and one of my mother's rings.

"So there was no man?"

No. She ransacked the house and hid those items somewhere. She was able to mail the money back to New York to my Aunt Bea, and asked her to hang on to it for her. I don't know whether Buss suspected her or not. She got away with it. One night she and I went for a ride. She had put the ring inside the camera, handed it to me and told me to toss it into a creek as we crossed over a bridge in Vinita. I did as I was told but was heartsick. I am not sure about the ring; it may have been one that my father had given her at one time. I did know that the camera was one that we had when my father was alive, and it was special to me. I often wondered if the creek ever got low enough for someone to have found it or is it still down there rusting away.

She got away with that, too. Sometime later (I didn't know of the deal until after it was done) she had found a house, got the money back from my aunt, put down a deposit and promised to buy this stucco-looking house at the north end of town. We would all go up there, usually on Sunday afternoons when Buss was home napping and my work was done, just to get away. Mother and I spent a lot of time just sitting at a picnic table, enjoying the outdoors, the trees and the peace away from him as the kids played.

I have to mention the times I tried to kill Buss besides the ones that involved the fighting. These were just me trying to get rid of him. There was one time when he was behind the washer doing some kind of repair. I was probably about sixteen. He had a beer, of course, open and sitting on top of the washer. Because I was standing in front of the washer and he was sitting on the floor behind it, I apparently was brave enough to reach up into the cupboard, get some rat poison and sprinkle some into his beer. He never saw me do it. He finished his can of beer, but nothing happened. I guess it wasn't enough.

"Were you really trying to kill him? Maybe you just wanted to make him sick."

Kill him, make him sick, I didn't care either way. Mostly I wanted him dead, though.

One time, while working in the market, our butcher,

Norman, watched me pull a cigarette from Buss's pack of Camels and insert a few pieces of red pepper deep into the cigarette. I put the cigarette back into the pack and resumed working. Sometime later that day I heard Buss coughing and choking pretty badly. Earlier I had seen him eating a popsicle and thought he was choking on that. I smiled and thought, "Good enough for you, pig." I heard him say in between catching his breath and coughing as he leaned over the sink, "That was a hot son-of-a-bitch, Norm." I had forgotten all about the laced cigarette. I got a little scared when he said, "Look in that cigarette, Norm." Everyone else just kept working, including me.

Now Norman was always trying to protect me somewhat, well, when he wasn't trying to grab me and kiss me when we both ended up in the cooler at the same time.

Norman used to tell me that I should come running out of the house when Buss was over there at the same time and have my blouse ripped open and to scream bloody murder. That would take care of him -- send him to jail. I couldn't do that because I'm not an actress. He would also tell me every night where the pin to the rifle that was used to shoot the animals for slaughter would be hidden. Buss made him start hiding it after my mother pointed it at him one night outside with me holding a knife and keeping him at bay.

"Oh my. What happened with the cigarette? Did you get caught?"

Well, I kept working but was pretty nervous as he and Norman kind of looked into the cigarette. Even though Norman watched me lace the cigarette, I knew he wouldn't betray me. He used a kind of gliding motion with his thumb and the red pepper grains fell to the floor as did the tobacco. He told me later how he did it so that nothing could be seen. But you know if you mix red pepper with tobacco it looks pretty much the same.

I tried that again several times after that but never knew if he ever choked again. Perhaps he was cautious after that and didn't suck so hard.

"What is the story on holding him at bay with knives and

guns?"

Well my mother actually had gone home to New York once. She used the excuse that one of her folks was dying. Wasn't true, and maybe she went back to get the four thousand dollars she sent back there. I don't know. Hell, I don't even know where I stayed while she was gone. Teresa may have gone with her. The rest of us must have stayed with Ruby. We had no family or close friends in Vinita. I believe innumerable amounts of stress caused me to forget many things.

"No doubt."

While mother was in New York she visited Buss's mother. There again, I don't know why she visited her, but I remember my mother telling me that his mother read Tarot cards. My mother let her read them for her. "There is danger around a white car." That is the only thing I remember my mother telling me about the reading.

One Sunday evening something started with them. I remember my mother with the rifle pointed at Buss and me a little ways over with a butcher knife while he was crouched down in front of our white Cadillac shielding himself from any harm. I know my mother wanted to pull that trigger. He kept yelling at her from behind the car. A car pulled up in front of the market and a woman got out. I walked over to her. I was all pumped up in some kind of survival mode. "May I help you?" I said a bit sarcastically. "You don't want to do this. I came home one day and saw my daddy dead," she said. "You don't want to do this." She didn't know how badly we did want to do this. I can't remember what else was said but she left pretty quickly. I guess she didn't call the cops or anything, no one came. I can't remember how long we carried this mission on until it was over nor do I remember how this one ended, just that it did and it was business as usual the next day.

About a week later I was in town and just about to enter a store when I heard someone say, "You Valentines better quit playing with those guns down there." I turned and saw about a ten year old boy hurrying off. That was a good indication how fast news traveled in this small town; we were sometimes the topic of conversations, children were listening and they knew who we were by sight. I was surprised and embarrassed.

One night mother and Buss had been fighting outside the market and I came around to see him holding her down in the gravel. I grabbed a hoe and hit him on the back. He got up and I ran. He had broken her collarbone that night.

Mother got a few licks in also at times. One time she slapped him in the face with a large piece of fresh cut round steak. Another time she took a butcher knife and cut across the top of his hand. Not deep enough for stitches, but it did leave a nasty scar.

That was one of the things that was so hard for me to understand. How could this insanity of fighting and wanting to kill each other go on as often as it did, and then the next day act as if nothing ever happened.

My mother and I use to sit outside sometimes talking about how we were going to kill Buss -- how we could kill him and cut him up as we did the cattle and hogs. How we could get rid of his bones by mixing them in with the animal bones that were picked up once a week. We could grind up the flesh and throw it into Bull Creek, the creek that ran behind the market.

What a hell of a thing to discuss with your daughter. We laughed though. We talked about these awful things to do to another human being and we laughed about it, a lot. One of the counselors that I told this to said, "The talking and laughing about it is probably what saved you from actually doing it."

That sounds as if mother and I got along well but we didn't, not really. I mean she was still always onto me. She continued to give me the third degree about Buss and I anytime we had been alone together for some reason. Although the third degree sessions had escalated in my teen years to more hitting and pulling my hair as if to produce an answer or a different one. Sometimes I would get a nose bleed from her slapping me on the left side of my face. One day I swore I would just keep my head over the tub until I bled to death, or so I hoped. I got in real trouble for accidentally losing one of Fred's diapers down the toilet when trying to clean it out. I got into trouble if the house wasn't in order or clean, even though we had the housekeepers, and I got into trouble if my sister and little brothers weren't happy, fed and preoccupied enough to stay out of the market.

I thought she would kill me the day Teresa fell off the horse and broke her arm, as if it were my fault; after all she was one of her favorites. I was always in trouble and always getting hit. I believe that is why I have a problem hearing out of my left ear and have bad sinus problems on the left side of my face. I was told once that my back wasn't developed enough to work and lift as I did since the age of nine or ten, and that is partly why I have back problems. Working in a meat market is not easy work, and especially when they expect you to lift seventy-five pound lugers of meat or grab half a hog and throw it onto a meat block, or a quarter of beef and do the same, and lift and carry hundreds of pounds of meat in and out of coolers and freezers all day, not to mention bent over cutting meat or packaging and wrapping meat all day. One time Buss made me pick up a one hundred pound barrel and lift it up onto another. I don't know how I did it but I did. One hundred pounds. I was a teenager.

"That is hard work."

Not only was I working hard in the market like a man, but Buss would try to rub up against me as he moved around from the cutting block to the cutting table or to the saw -- any chance he had. The work was hard and stressful; the harassment was almost unbearable. When I almost reached a crazy place, I would go up into a little storage area in the market over the cutting area and I would estimate where Buss was standing at the cutting block. There were some of those washer motors that we brought from NY up there and I wanted to drop one onto him. It was an action that called for no mistakes -- no miscalculation and it had to kill him. After much thought I couldn't be sure of the end result so I never carried out the deed.

Many, many times I would lay out in the dirt in the field behind the house and aim the rifle at Buss as he walked from the market to the house, finger on the trigger, but never pulling it.

"I can't imagine living like that."

Well then, there was our employee, Norman, who also was trying to get grabby with me all the time. I had no one to tell about what was going on with me: the sexual harassment, the abuse.

There was this one woman in her twenties named Johnny who worked at the local drug store. I thought I could tell her something, but I didn't. I hung out at the store because she was so pretty and seemed so happy. I could tell she was a good person and it was just so refreshing to be around her. Everyone loved her, and her laughter and personality -- contagious.

I remember calling her a few times from home when I was really upset but never mentioned what was going on. I think I expected her to know and ask me. Kids don't know what to do or at least not then. I mean what could anyone do even if I had told someone about even one of the things I was dealing with. If it were today, we would have all been taken away from that situation, but at that time I doubt it.

Many years later and when I was an adult, Johnny and I talked about my teen years. She revealed that she thought that something was going on with me and felt bad for me, but didn't know what to do. She also wrote to me expressing that she remembered a pretty, uptight miserable young girl. She continued with, "I felt such compassion for you and could do nothing for you. Of course you never told me why you were so miserable but I guessed."

Johnny also mentioned in the letter that she remembered my brother Don as "this good looking kid who seemed happy, didn't show his emotions like you did."

"That is a lot for a young girl to have to live with and go through."

Yes, well and I worked right alongside my mother and I protected her and kept her secrets and loved her and she treated me like shit. She couldn't have loved me or even liked me for that matter, but she expected me to be there for her and do everything she told me to do without question. I was as true and loyal as a mistreated dog.

"Perhaps it was the alcohol. How often did she drink?"

Every chance she got. When she went to the grocery store she would buy beer and I had to hide it in the house. What I called her brewery was a place under a drawer in one of the bedrooms. There was always a good supply kept there. When she would somehow go to the house during the day from working in the market, she would drink a little. Buss would drink his beer out in the open all day long in the market or in the house, but she wasn't allowed to drink. She would get mean; correction -- meaner when she would drink too much. Maybe her life was a bit tolerable when she drank off and on during the day.

At night when we were all watching a show on TV, mother would look at me and give me a signal with her hand, kind of like sipping something. That meant for me to get up and go into the bedroom which was right next to the living room. If I didn't do it correctly, Buss would have heard me pull out the whole drawer, get a can of beer out and make sure the others didn't roll, put the drawer back quietly, and take the beer into the bathroom. As I popped it open, I would have to cough at the same time so he couldn't hear the flip tab.

"Oh my. How often did that happen?"

All the time just as everything else happened all the time: the fighting, the drinking, the abuse, the work, the stress, the dysfunction and secrets. Pure ugliness and evil existed in our lives and it was Satan. Satan lived at our house.

There were times when I just wanted it to end. The ugliness had to end. I realized when my father died, just how much life could change just by someone dying, and I didn't care who died. If just one of them would go, it would all change again. Even though one was my mother, I wished and prayed that one of them would kill the other when they fought or they both could die for that matter.

"Your mother? Was that because she was so cruel to you?"

Maybe or maybe she was driving me mad or the whole life situation was making me crazy with rage sometimes and death seemed like the only way out. Don't think I didn't think about killing myself because I had, many times, but I also believed it was a sin to do that. I thought about running away at times but where could I have gone, and then, too, how would any of them survive without me?

CHAPTER SIX

I remember in tenth grade, I was called into the counselor's office. My grades were pretty bad. "What's going on?" Mrs. Parkhurst asked. First of all, I didn't like this woman. Everyone else did, but not me. I found this to be the norm. I never seemed to be like everyone else, but I was perfectly okay with being different. In fact I felt like I was right and everyone else just didn't see the things that I saw and I accepted both my views and myself. So, Mrs. Parkhurst seemed too authoritative with kind of a cocky attitude, two things that I have never been able to tolerate. I could have been wrong about her but this is how I felt. Maybe I was just a bit defensive, who knows.

I sat wanting to tell her of the child slavery that I was subjected to since around age nine. How my daily schedule was now -- up at six a.m. to sweep and mop the front of the market. Every day, spray out the gut wrenching rags that were used to wipe off the meat. Then I had to pick them up from the slaughterhouse floor and try to wring them out somewhat, which would make me literally gag. Then I would take them to the house to put in the washer. If there was nothing else too pressing, I could then get ready for school, all the while, my brothers and sister, running around and trying to help them get ready for the day also.

I also didn't tell her how hard it was to fit in some homework every night because of my duties and how until this very year I would try to get two hours sleep before having to clean the market after midnight. This was about the time mother and Buss would come to the house after their eighteen hour day. Before Don moved out, this was one of our duties and most nights it took us two hours to clean.

And even though we always had a housekeeper, my

mother would make me pick up and clean up the house before they would get there. Guess my mother still wanted us to look like the perfect little family -- all clean and tidy. I know it was a lot of work for me.

"Sounds like it."

So I wanted to continue telling the counselor that after school I had to watch my brothers and sister. Cater to their every whim so that they wouldn't go to the market and tell on me, which meant I wasn't doing my job in keeping them occupied and out of the market. I fed them supper which most times were TV Dinners because I couldn't cook. I had never been taught but just as well because I didn't want to learn anyway. My mother never had the time to teach me because she was always working. But as I say, it would have just been one more thing expected of me.

I can cook pretty well now but I used to be a bit dangerous in the kitchen; a bit clumsy; have had fires burst from the oven and pans on the stove. Mostly from being in a hurry I think. I also leave drawers and cabinets open. There were times when I would have been in the kitchen cooking and after leaving it, noticed several cupboards and drawers open and would have to go back and close everything. Over the years I have realized that the more stressed I was, the more drawers and cupboards would be open.

So I didn't tell Mrs. Parkhurst anything about how my life really was. I don't know what I told her, probably just listened to her or half listened because I really didn't care. I remember asking her a question in psychology class once, don't remember what it was now, but at the time I thought it was pretty smart of me to ask her believing she couldn't answer it. She said something like me being quiet most of the year and then coming up with a great question like that, perhaps I needed to research the answer. All I wanted that day was to see if she knew the answer. I was being a smart ass.

CHAPTER SEVEN

My senior year I was living at the hidey house most of the time alone and had access to mother's booze. I often attended my senior year daily with a buzz. I was buzzed in the morning and then again at noon because I would go home for lunch. I had a shorthand class in the morning and my friend, Christy, sat across from me. A time or two she would wave her hand across her face to indicate she could smell the booze. I remember trying to decipher the silly script out loud when called on to do so and my classmates were laughing, but I was laughing with them. What was worse was my afternoon class of bookkeeping was with the same teacher, Mrs. Butler. No wonder I didn't learn anything. But I just wanted to finish school -- never to return. I wanted to work and make money and maybe one day have a life of my own. I wanted to make movies and also thought about joining the Peace Corps.

I didn't make very good grades in junior high or high school. How could I? Besides now there is a name for it. I was pretty much an ADD kid. School requires a lot of memory work for which I lack the ability to retain almost anything unless I do it over and over again. And I really couldn't get algebra no matter how hard I tried. It made no sense to me whatsoever. I muddled through, but failed second semester of algebra two and had to take it over again my senior year in order to graduate.

That's when this coach/teacher who had the hots for me told me that he passed me with a "D-" so I could graduate, but I really didn't even make that. I was very grateful of course, and even happier to know that I had such an effect on him without having to perform any kind of sexual gratitude. I heard many years later that he did get caught with a young girl in the lockers.

I enjoyed my journalism class taught by Emma Rose Moore. When we were assigned the task of writing a short story, my desire for writing came out and the pen speedily glided across the paper keeping up with my imagination. I felt pretty proud that I also got a by-line or two for the school newspaper that year.

Well, I managed to graduate. Cap and gown on and diploma in hand but no family members to see me walk on the stage to receive it. At the end of the ceremony, classmates and their families were in the hallways; lots of hugs and congratulations going on. Someone asked me where my mother was and I answered, "Oh, around here somewhere," as I pretended to look for her. Afterwards I met up with some graduating friends at the local pizza place. Even though I was invited to a party, I didn't go because there was talk of swimming and I wasn't comfortable with my body.

Mother and Buss had gone to Don's graduation. I remember taking a picture of them all dressed up. It would have been nice of mother to attend mine even though I wouldn't have really wanted either of them there. They might have shown up drunk. I know Don was at the house earlier that evening because I have pictures, but he must have gone back to college because he wasn't at my graduation either. Oh well, I had my own car, was living at the hidey house, working at the market and finally drawing a salary making really good money. Now I was finished with high school.

I was so happy to be finished with school. I hated it, hated it, hated it, and when my mother asked me once during my senior year if I wanted to go to college or work, without hesitation I said work. Secretly wanting to become a great writer and movie maker; I never told anyone of my dreams for fear of ridicule and discouragement.

After graduation I was making a little more than minimum wage, and would always have two or three hundred dollars in hand. Should have been putting it in the bank for my future because I don't know where it all went. Maybe I could have escaped, gone to California and pursued my dreams. Who am I trying to kid? I couldn't get away from my family, couldn't leave them. They needed me. Mother had some kind of hold on me and she and those kids depended on me for everything. I was their security, their strength and problem solver. There were many nights that I slept with a gun and knife in my bed in order to protect my family from Buss. I was always on guard even as I tried to sleep. My sister, even to this day feels better just knowing I am close by. Of course, Grace (mother) needed me for her accomplice, her go-to girl, her punching bag, but also her strength, and clean up girl.

"It sounds like she needed a lot of help."

Somehow this woman, my mother, made me love her unconditionally. She got me to do whatever she wanted -- no matter what it was. She made me loyal to her. She trusted I would always do the right thing and never turn on her. Wow, what a friend I was to her. But she wasn't much of a friend or a mother to me.

CHAPTER EIGHT

It was very hard to keep my heart in check. There was so much ugliness going on. I so wanted to keep my relationship with God close to my heart even though I had bad thoughts and actions.

There was this one time I had gone to some religious revival. It might have been Seventh Day Adventist, not sure, and I think it lasted for several evenings. One week when I was eighteen and out of school, I went by myself. I was quite inspired and had some feeling within me like nothing I had ever felt before. I can't explain it; I just know it was there, within me. Maybe that is what they call "filled with the Holy Spirit." I have never felt that since.

"What happened to that feeling?"

Well, as with everything in my life, something ugly happened. I lost my temper and lost the feeling. Lost the holiness.

I remember going home to the hidey house after one of those revival meetings. My mother was there and the kids because she and Buss had had a fight as usual. I can't remember what her injury was but I lost my temper, foul language came out of my mouth and murderous thoughts were running through my mind. I drove to the meat market, sat in my car close by contemplating what horrible act I could do to him.

My point was that I had one of the most beautiful experiences in my life and then it was gone in an instant, thanks to Satan.

This wasn't the first time mother came to that house after they had a fight. She would bounce back and forth from one place to the other.

I had been gone from the house and Buss had come up there. He and mother had got into a fight. Somehow he had pushed her onto the bed and the bed rails broke and the mattress was on the floor. Anyway, I came home to her crying and bitching about them fighting. I lost my temper and lifted each mattress and each bedrail one by one, carried them through the house and tossed them out into the back yard. The bad thing was that I was a few months pregnant this time. Then my sister and our friends, Doris and Jennie, were either there or I drove over to their house, picked them up and I drove to the meat market. My sister was really mad, too. She was only twelve at that time, but seemed so much older.

We drove by the market. My sister wanted to get out and break the windows. She and Jennie were dropped off. The plan was for them to do the deed and then run toward the creek bridge several hundred feet away. Doris and I would pick them up there.

It was the funniest thing I have ever seen. They broke the windows with rocks. They took off running. I was driving very slowly toward the bridge. I could see Buss come out of the market to see who had broken the windows. Teresa and Jennie had run to the bridge and literally dove down into the bank of the creek and somehow climbed up to the other side. Doris and I had the back doors open to the car and they jumped in as I sped away.

Funny there seemed to be no other cars on the road, which was actually a highway, Route 66 to be exact. It was night but not that late. I drove to this other house that my mother had rented for storage. We hid out there in the backyard talking and laughing about the whole incident and listening for any sirens. There were none. We had gotten away with it.

"I can't believe you lifted the mattresses and rails and tossed them out while pregnant."

I had a very bad temper when pushed too far. I could take a lot, but there was that breaking point. My mother, in later years, probably when I was in my late forties, used to say, "You have the patience of Job." One of the good things she said of me, oh and the other was, when I would say I was fat, she would say, "You're not fat, you're just a big girl." Then again this was when I was in my late forties. Then she would continue with, "Now, so & so, now she's fat, that is fat!" Showing me comparison.

But as for my temper, my mother knew what buttons to push to get me there -- whether it got directed toward her or she wanted it directed toward someone else. I can remember instances where I could hear a hum in my head as I would be swearing and cussing and hitting the wall or counters or something. It was as if it wasn't even me. I often thought that this could be what an insane or crazy person experiences when committing unspeakable acts. Perhaps they hear a humming in their head and maybe not aware of what they are really doing.

"So you mentioned being pregnant. You hadn't been turned off by men?"

Surprisingly, no. I always, and I mean as long as I can remember, liked boys. There were a few boys that liked me in grade school and also in high school. You know how grade school goes -- you like each other, but the only thing going on or should be is book carrying, walking home from school together and hanging out at school. At least, that's all that ever went on when and where I went to grade school. In high school, well, I wasn't allowed to date so that didn't give me any opportunities to really get to know any boys.

There was one boy named Mark who liked me when I was in ninth grade. He broke up with his girlfriend only to find a scared girl who could hardly talk to him and was afraid her mother was going to drive by the school and see us talking, so he eventually moved on.

I really liked this one boy who was a couple of years older than me. Eddie. He played drums in his band and they dressed in suits. He was part or all Native American. He looked like Engelbert Humperdinck to me -- very handsome. He drove a Corvette and had come over to the house once or twice and we sat in the car and talked, and we talked at school. But that is as far as that went. I guess we were going to meet at Teen Town, a place for teens to dance one Friday night. He called the market and told my mother to tell me he couldn't make it.

I guess she thought I was trying to be sneaky, and maybe I

was. I think it was more like I was going and he was going and maybe we would have run into each other. That call really set her off. She came over to the house, yelled and screamed at me. She slapped me across the face a few times, screaming, yelling and pulling my hair, and then she actually started to choke me. We went down together onto the three stairs that led to a loft like bedroom, and she was on top of me, strangling me. I almost didn't care. I sometimes wished she would kill me. It was like a scene from the movie, Mommy Dearest, about Joan Crawford.

"How old were you?"

Tenth grade.

"Old enough to date, maybe."

Well, apparently not for me. I remember when I was about nine or ten. My mother and I were outside, seems like it was fall or the beginning of winter. We were probably walking back from the store. I can see it clearly in my mind. We were almost to the house when she said, "If you ever get pregnant, I'll break both your legs." I don't remember any conversation that lead up to that statement nor anything after. All I know is I was terrified. I didn't even know how you got pregnant. I was terrified thinking, "What if you like a boy and he likes you, will I get pregnant? What if you like a boy and you touch hands? Will I get pregnant?" I was pretty stupid.

"No, you were a child. A child whose mother never talked to you about life."

I didn't know anything about sex, not even into my high school years. I started to learn from my younger brothers and sister when they were talking and laughing about certain things. They were 8, 10 and 13 years younger than me. How could that be? I know, I was so traumatized because of Buss trying to molest me for years, my mother letting him try and with that statement in the back of my mind, not to mention the other dirty old men, I simply did not choose to think of sex. I am surprised I even had a healthy sex life once I started. Well pretty much a healthy one, except when I went through the "I hate men period in my life." And speaking of periods, I don't really remember my mother explaining that too well, either. She showed me how to put those ugly, gross, huge pads on by hooking them up with those garter like belts. Those were the most disgusting things to have to wear on top of having periods.

I experienced terrible migraines with my periods also, but my mother always said it was in my head. I was very sick. I would throw up and have diarrhea on top of the headache and terrible cramps. She didn't believe me and made me get up, go to school, work or whatever I needed to do. She had no mercy whatsoever. She never had them, so therefore they didn't exist. She never took me to the doctor. She simply did not care and didn't believe me. I would be sick for three hours or more before I would start to feel a little better. I think now, maybe that is why I view being sick as a sign of weakness. I am rarely sick and feel that I can't reveal anything to anyone without looking weak.

I discovered tampons when I was about eighteen but really didn't know how to use them. Looked at the instructions but didn't understand that they actually were to be inserted. What a mental block I had about such things.

"You must have been pretty sheltered also. Didn't you have a social life? Girl friends?"

I worked a lot. Babysat my brothers and sister. I did belong to a club called Sophisticated Skirts in high school and I was in the Pep Club. But I don't think sex was the topic of our conversations. I had one really good friend since the ninth grade, but she was a little lady like me. We are still friends to this day -- my best friend, Vinnie.

CHAPTER NINE

I was almost nineteen, still a virgin and just started to have some freedom. A couple of friends and I heard about these boys that were moving to Vinita from California. When they arrived it was summer and we all met while hanging around the city pool. They were both cute but poor I found out soon enough. Ron was older than his brother Tom, but he was still two years younger than I. Ron was sweet although sometimes sweet can be mistaken for not real intelligent. He was really good in math though, but his folks didn't seem too intelligent either.

So you are probably wondering how a rich girl got involved with this poor boy from the other side of the tracks.

Well, one night I was out driving around town, "Dragging Main." I pulled into the car wash to wash my car. It was an early, dark evening. Some man, of course, pulled in with his Cadillac convertible, an older man, sporting a ponytail trying to be younger, tried to pick me up. I lied, told him I had a boyfriend and that I was going to the library. He didn't care, yadda yadda yadda, take me for a ride, etc., etc. I did manage to leave in my own car and drove over to Ron's house. We talked, I told him about the man and we went riding around, "Dragging Main" and there you have it.

Ron and I started dating soon after that night. We dated for about a year and a half before I got pregnant, wasn't taking birth control. My mother said, "Nice going, George" when I told her. Ron was immature, lazy and knew nothing about responsibility, and he liked the girls. His parents didn't like me, well his dad did, but not in a good way if you know what I mean.

"Did he make advances toward you?"

Of course, I never knew a man that didn't until I was in

my forties, and then it was only two men. Anyway, mother hated Ron and his family. They were white trash to her and, well, they kind of were.

Jim, Buss's first son had served his time in Vietnam and had returned home. Either he got in contact with his dad or vice versa. So at some point Jim had come to Vinita and had lived with us for a while and then got married and continued to work in the meat market.

One day he came to the hidey house because for some reason there was no electricity on one side of the house. Also for some reason, my family was staying there at this time. Mother and Buss were probably fighting and, after all, it was an escape house. I could see from the window some sparks that looked like white lightning come from where Jim was standing outside checking the fuse box. He got the electricity working but sometime around midnight that very night I awoke to a throat full of smoke. I hurried to my mother's room to wake her. I thought the smoke was coming from the basement because I could see it rising from the floor vent in the hall. After waking mother, I continued to make my way out and glanced toward the bedroom where my brothers slept. Luckily all my younger siblings were spending the night with friends because I saw tiny flames burning their way up the blanket on one of the beds. I managed to call for help before exiting the house. Mother must have called Buss because I remember him standing outside with us watching the firemen do their job. I could never understand how it happened. I know the bed was somewhat pushed up to the wall and I knew there was a plug in there, but how did the blanket catch fire from the wall plug in. You would think a piece of the blanket would have to be in the socket. It was very odd, and I never did hear how the fire got started. Of course mother suspected Jim.

I prayed so hard and so much that Buss would never set eyes on my child. I thanked God when he died 20 days before her birth.

I started to have some pains. Our friend Doris climbed through the window of my bedroom at our hidey house as she often did to visit. She told me I was having contractions. I didn't think so at first so moved to the living room couch. My brother Don came over and he suspected the same thing. He was excited and began to drop rose petals on me. As the day went on I believed it became time to go to the hospital. I labored long. Twenty-four hours in all.

The nurses knew who I was, that "Valentine girl," which the town people referred to me as. I asked them to keep it quiet that I was there, after all I was not married. It didn't bother me that much because I was twenty one, and I didn't care much about what people thought, but I still wanted my privacy.

My mother showed up in the labor room, drunk and I yelled, "Get her out of here," as I designated where the door was with my arm. One elderly nurse would come in periodically and report that the waiting room was full of my friends, and that there had been calls, but she said, "But I have been telling them, no publicity, no publicity." Another nurse came in and asked me if I wanted Ron to come into the labor room with me. I did of course want him in there, but at some point had wished he wasn't because he wouldn't shut up.

Ron had a photographic memory, so as I encountered labor pain after labor pain, I had to listen to him telling me about movies in detail that he really enjoyed. One thing that surprised me was that he actually thought to bring me my rosary beads.

I had my beautiful, perfect daughter at eight o'clock the next morning on a Monday. There was another girl in the room with me, and the nurses said they were going to bring our babies in to us. I assumed they would bring mine first because I was furthest away from the door. When I saw a nurse enter the room holding this first baby with its dark hair almost standing straight up, I knew that one was not mine. Soon they brought my daughter to me. As they walked over to me, I started to feel this overwhelming love within me and chills throughout my body. She was perfect and beautiful and she was already trying to hold her head up. I knew then that she would be a strong, healthy human, and I prayed I would be a much better mother than mine. I wanted to protect her from all the bad.

CHAPTER TEN

Buss's death brought a lot of turmoil and a lot of unfinished business. I have found out over the years, a selfish man leaves a mess behind for others to deal with, and usually leaves nothing of value. They do and live as they want. To hell with anyone else, ever!

There was a viewing in Vinita, and although I hated seeing dead people, I had to go see this. I had to actually see that he was dead, in a casket, not breathing, gone for good. Never to rise again. Deader than dead. I even wanted to stick a big pin in his arm to make sure. I couldn't believe that terror had ended. After the viewing in Vinita, my mother and two younger brothers flew back to New York with the body to bury him.

While she was gone, Jim had himself appointed executor of the estate, so when my mother got back to Oklahoma, she was pretty much ousted from the meat market. We still had our hidey house so we all stayed there. I had to get a job. I had a baby and a new car to pay for. I believe my mother was given some kind of allotment from the business for my two brothers until social security checks started for them. So the only job available for me was cleaning a motel. I was humiliated, but you do what you have to do sometimes, and also that's what a rich girl gets for loving a poor boy. Apparently Ron was not going to work. Didn't know how lazy he was at first but found out soon enough.

Soon mother began the process of trying to get the meat market back. She hired this high dollar lawyer who took, in my opinion, more than was called for in fees. Because I confronted him on several issues, he asked that I not attend the meetings. Here again, my opinion, but I think he knew that I knew he was a crook. We had to go to court to establish the fact that mother and Buss were still acting as man and wife when he passed away to make mother the executor of the estate.

Sometime after the hearings, Ron and I ran off to Missouri to get married because he was only nineteen and needed parents' permission in Oklahoma, but not in Missouri. I didn't even know that's what we were going to do that day. Ron had a habit of just wanting to go for a ride out of town so that day it was Missouri. I didn't know he found out he could marry without parents' permission there and we had already gotten blood tests. We found a church, a pastor and two witnesses off the street; sisters that were more than happy to attend our little wedding. My daughter was two months old and in my arms as we were pronounced husband and wife.

When Ron's parents found out we had gone to Missouri and had gotten married, they were mad -- his mother especially. We had kept it a secret for a couple of months. I guess his parents didn't mind that I occasionally slept with him in their house unwed, but when Ron blabbed that we were married his mother went ballistic.

I was holding my daughter and his mother got up and came over to me and starting hitting me and yelling. So we left that night and stayed at the motel where I had been working. We decided to run off to California. I got my paycheck the next morning. I remember it was $65.00. That is what we left with. $65.00!

I am ashamed to say, I left my four month old daughter with my mother for about two weeks, but she survived. I can't believe I did that, but thought it was the best thing to do at the time. I had no idea what would or could have happened as Ron and I set out to start a life together. The plan was to get to California, get him started to work and I would come back to get her.

Ron's father asked if they could keep her! This was after they said the baby was not Ron's. This, after his mother had a male nurse at the hospital tell her the blood type of my daughter to prove it wasn't Ron's. He had the nerve to ask if they could keep my daughter after his wife called me names and beat on me.

I could have had that nurse fired. The blood type was

AB+. I am B+, Ron A+. I was fortunate that it came out that simple for them to believe. I think it was the blood type that may have almost convinced them that she was their son's daughter. I remember in biology a chart that showed different combinations of blood types combined and the blood type an offspring could end up with. Had our types been different and came out confusing (as they appeared on that chart), well, his parents would have never been convinced the child was his. But with an A+ & B+= AB+, even their ignorant, uneducated, white trash existence could understand A + B = AB!

Ron wanted me to let them take her, but I refused.

Our trip going out to California was quite uneventful. We both took turns driving my '66 Mustang. Wish I had kept that car. I almost let us run out of gas once in the desert. We did sleep in the car a few hours a couple of times at rest stops. I guess you could say I started roughing it once I met Ron.

We stayed with my father's sister, Mary. Her husband, Doug, had given Ron a job at his service station. I took a bus back to Vinita to get my daughter. By the time I got there, my legs were swollen pretty badly. I saw the doctor, grabbed my daughter and was back on the bus the same day returning to California. I don't recommend any of that.

One day, Ron just took off to a town where he used to live instead of showing up to work. When he got back he told me he looked up an old girlfriend and basically got run out of town by her new boyfriend.

I was hurt but this wasn't his first time to be an idiot. Ron was a very immature person. I really didn't know what to do. There we were, trying to make a new start to our lives with a baby, and I really wanted to live in California but I knew we couldn't stay with relatives for very long. He, of course, said he was sorry and that he loved me, etc., etc.

Mother was awarded the market back while I was gone. I think we were in California for a couple of months when I called home to the meat market to talk to my mother. I ended up talking to Norman; the one who always made passes at me. He begged me to come back. "We're running our legs off here and need your help."

I thought about it. It didn't look like Ron was going to work, even though my uncle had given him a job, and I think he wanted to go back to Oklahoma. I figured I could do more in Oklahoma to support us than in beautiful Huntington Beach.

Our drive back to Oklahoma was rough. The car broke down in Flagstaff, Arizona. It was snowing, and for some reason the heater was not working either. It was dark and snowing pretty hard. I remember pushing the car until my lungs felt like they were going to burst. A tow truck driver happened to see us and towed us into Flagstaff. Turns out it was the alternator. Then again in Shamrock, Texas, the bell housing fell out of the transmission. The shifter just seemed to break off in Ron's hands.

"Oh no. How was the baby during all this?"

She was good; I had her wrapped up warm with blankets. We had to try to hitch a ride. Ron wasn't getting anyone to stop. I got out of the car with my baby in arms and a family in a Honda stopped to help us. We were all cramped in the car, but I was very thankful.

They actually drove us to Oklahoma City where they just kind of dropped us off at a motel. I didn't know anything about Oklahoma City, and didn't want to inconvenience them any further. My brother, Don, lived in Norman but worked at one of the radio stations in Oklahoma City, about a 45 minute drive from city to city, so I knew I could call him.

We sat in this motel until he was able to come pick us up. He took us to his apartment in Norman. My daughter and I stayed there while he and Ron drove back to Shamrock, Texas, and towed the car back to Norman.

The next day, Don towed and carted us back to Vinita. He got pulled over once for not having lights on the Mustang. He got really mad and raised his voice to the officer. Don had a quick temper and it was uncalled for, but he was probably stressing somewhat having to get us back to Vinita.

"So you made it back to Vinita, then what happened?"

Well, we stayed at a motel until my mother signed for a loan at the bank for a house that we intended to buy. I went back to work at the meat market.

I assessed the situation and found out that my mother was not really working in the market. She was pretty much staying upstairs in the apartment with her boyfriend, Eldon, and drinking. She had hired a few new people. There was a lot of work to do. The cooler was full of custom meat to be cut, processed and wrapped. Also, this was a very busy business. People would come from Tulsa, Kansas, and the Grand Lake area to buy our meat, not to mention catering to all of the restaurants around the lake and town of Vinita. But at this time, the stepbrother had opened his own meat market in town and we were no longer selling meat over the counter We had lost several restaurants to him because he was selling the meat cheaper. So it was mainly custom killing and processing.

I had to let a few people go because I took the place of them. I told my mother that I was going to dock pay from one of our meat cutters when he wouldn't show up.

Although I liked Charlie, business was business, and I was trying to save this one. He was an alcoholic, and this was one alcoholic I could control by not paying him for not working. I also had to let two part-time men go who cleaned the market at night because I could see we couldn't continue to pay them.

Walter and Rat. Rats' name was really Virgil. I don't know why he was called Rat. They were black as were some of our other employees that we considered almost like family. They worked during the day at a Ford dealership in Vinita, both mechanics. They both had been with us for years, but we could no longer afford to pay them.

Walter had been in a bad car accident at one time, walked with kind of a limp and a bit of a dragging of his leg and had lost the use of one of his arms. I heard they wanted to cut it off but he wouldn't let them. He had learned to use that arm for many things. He was very strong and could do anything. I hated to have to let him go, he was a very sweet man. Very loyal, kind and a great worker. I trusted Walter.

Virgil, on the other hand, although never did anything to make me distrust him, I didn't. I could never hear what he was saying, he talked very softly. I don't know if he talked like that to everyone or just to me when he was trying to say something dirty to me. I just tried to ignore him. It was very strange but I can remember him trying to say dirty things to me since I met him and grinning as he was talking. As in any situation with men, I didn't tell anyone about it nor did I know how to stop it. I just tried to avoid the situations when they came up and they came up often.

I told my mother that her boyfriend, Eldon, and his buddy could clean the market. I let Ron work there, probably so I could keep an eye on him, and to basically start him in the working world for which he had no clue.

"I thought it was a thriving business...?"

It was. We were very wealthy in a sense. When Buss died we found out that he had a false corporation, crooked bookkeeper and he owed back taxes for about five years. Then after going through court on who should be the Administrator and the lawyers' fees, and after Jim turned the market back over to my mother, there was no money in the bank, etc. So then it became an uphill battle trying to keep everything and everyone paid until we lost the battle. Also true to Buss's practices, he had about a hundred twenty thousand dollars cash hidden somewhere. I always suspected that Jim found it the night Buss died or soon after, or it could have been Rat.

Rat had told mother and I that Buss had him carry the money around in the trunk of his car, but had hidden it somewhere in the market before he died. According to Rat, Buss intended to put it into a trust fund for my brothers, Mark and Fred.

"What made him decide to put money into a trust fund? Doesn't sound like him."

Oh, possibly after he had open heart surgery. He had the best heart surgeon at that time, Dr. Cooley in Houston -- a Triple bypass. That was pretty new and major surgery in 1972. They said he had apparently had many heart attacks throughout the years because his heart was very scarred up. Thing is they told him he would have to stop working; drinking, smoking and eating like a pig. Buss didn't stop doing any of those things, and then he even started to smoke pot. Needless to say he only lived a year after the surgery.

The night he died, my mother had made him dinner and they had sex. He dropped dead, plain and simple. Where was the suffering, God? How did he get to die like that while others, good people, suffer? He died up over the market where he had built and furnished an elaborate home for all of us, he thought. Living room, family room, kitchen and dining room, four bedrooms, three bathrooms. Each bathroom had TV and phone jacks and the master bathroom had a sunken tub. None of us really ever lived there with him. Mother was back and forth from the other house as were the boys. Teresa and I lived at the other house as I said, my senior year.

"You never knew what happened to the money?"

The night Buss died, Rat and Walter were downstairs cleaning the market. Rat said Jim went looking for the money. Mother and the boys were brought to the other house by the funeral director. I, pregnant, was lying on the couch when the boys came in sort of crying. They stood by me for a moment and I asked what was wrong and Fred said, "It's not funny, George, dad's dead." I couldn't believe it, sat up and asked where mother was. I looked out the window and saw her getting out of the car. Mark and Fred were the same age as Don and I were when our father died.

My mother came in and told me to go to the funeral home and make sure he was dead.

"And you did?"

I did and they said he was. I couldn't believe it but was elated.

Well, I never did kill Buss although I did put a hit out on Eldon, my mother's then new boyfriend. God, I hated that man.

He was about eighteen years younger than my mother. He smoked pot and he didn't work. I don't know what she was thinking. I know what she drunkenly repeated several times, "When Buss died, they all thought they would get me."

"What did that mean?"

It meant that she thought the men in Vinita would want to be with her after Buss's death, and that she would have ended up a wealthy woman with the market and everything. Not all the men, just a few certain ones that may have at one time or another shown some interest. So in her mind, by choosing this young guy from out of town would show them, show them what? I have no idea because he was worthless. Even though she would always say, "Eldon is a good man." Compared to who? Buss? Maybe she wanted to take a controlling position now.

"Did you follow through with the hit?"

Oh yes, this is how that all went down. Apparently I had expressed my feelings of hate to Rat. He told me he had connections in Kansas City. I told him let's do this.

"Kill Eldon?"

No, I told Rat I just wanted him run out of town. Rat said, "They'll hang him by his eyeballs." I insisted that I did not want that.

"How old were you?"

I was almost twenty three. So the agreement was that they scare him and run him out of town. I was unaware that Rat may have had his own agenda at that time also because other men were taken care of that night as well as those that were associated with mother.

Mother and Buss got a divorce about a year or so before his death. She began dating this man named Bobby. He wanted to marry my mother but because he had two sons she said it would never work. What would never work in my opinion was that this man had nothing and liked to drink also.

So she got this call. Bobby had been run off the road and beaten up pretty badly. He told her he was told to stay away from her. That same night, Norman got his leg broken at a bar by someone.

I remember my mother crying and telling me to "Call them off, call them off." I don't know if I told her or how she found out I was behind the deal. But I wasn't behind all of it. Bobby wasn't a threat. I wasn't worried about him. And I wouldn't have hurt Norman. I had no reason at that time. I told her I wouldn't call them off. I wanted Eldon gone. She kept begging me.

The next day a friend of the family, Wilma, called to tell me that she had seen the men from Kansas City. I assume mother told her. They had gone into a bar where she happened to be and so was Eldon. She said there were three large black men dressed in suits. They started toward Eldon, but he ran out of the bar and had run down to, there again, that creek -- Bull Creek. He had gotten away. I asked Rat what the hell happened? He said they had to catch the plane back to Kansas City. They should have gotten to him the night before. He had warning. Needless to say I was very disappointed. I did vow to never do that again though. The first one was a favor. The second may have come with commitments or consequences.

News travels in a small town. About a year or so later I was asked by some of Ron's friends if I had had our ex-lawyer killed. I hadn't and had not even thought of it, even though he embarrassed me and made me mad on the witness stand during the hearing to determine who should be executor of Buss's estate.

"What happened at the hearing?"

Jack was our lawyer until Buss died and then Jim hired him. Jack basically turned against mother and I.

I was pregnant but not married at the time of the hearing, and Jack was trying to discredit mother by not being legally married to Buss. They were common law. But the courts allowed them to get a divorce and then they got back together. He was trying to show the courts that they weren't really married and that

Jim should be the executor. Jack said something to the fact that I was pregnant, but not married -- something like my mother and Buss's situation in that she had children but had never legally married Buss. It required an answer and I replied, "Yeah, I guess so."

Months later Jack apologized to mother and me for going to the other side. And some time later, word was that he had gotten run off a bridge on his way home. His car landed upside down in the creek and he drowned. It wasn't me though. I liked Jack and his wife. I felt strange though the night mother and I went to visit his wife. As I sat there, I wondered if she had heard anything about me and my Italian-like hits. It was a very small town and seemed like people heard everything. I hoped she hadn't heard whatever rumor was going on about me having Jack run off the road.

CHAPTER ELEVEN

Buss was dead. I was trying to run the market at twenty two, twenty three. I had talked to some of the restaurant owners at the lake and they were willing to come back to us. Mother was rarely seen. She spent her time upstairs in the living quarters or occasionally at a bar with Eldon and other friends drinking the days and nights away.

I was aware that mother and Eldon would get into some kind of squabbles, and I know that one day I pointed a rifle at him and told him to leave. I was very angry about a fight they had, but I kept control. He did leave for a few days but mother let him come back. Another time they had had a fight and she said he pulled her back and she somehow cut her arm on the bed rails that had some jagged edges on them. This was in the bedroom that Buss had died in. It was bad enough that she needed stitches. When the bandages came off and healed over, there was a distinctive scar in the shape of a large V.

I went to Eldon's brother's house, a Seventh Day Adventist Preacher, and you should have heard the language that came from my mouth. I called Eldon everything in the book and didn't care what his brother thought or his wife who was listening from behind the staircase. I told him he better get his brother or I was going to kill him. Believe it or not, a few months after that mother ended up getting cut on the same arm in the same way. When it had healed over, there were two more V's. They were all connected. A large V, a small one and then the other just a little smaller than the large one. The significant prophetic statement that Buss made to mother at one time was, "If I ever catch you with another man I will brand you." And there you have it. The three V's for his name, Vincent Victor Valentine. Satan at work.

While I was trying to keep the business going and keeping

it all together again because of mother's choices, my younger brothers and sister were doing whatever they wanted. Mark and Fred walked out of Walmart once with a blow up rowboat that they did not purchase. They said they took it to the creek which ran behind the market and played with it until they put a hole in it. They took it back to Walmart and got money back for it. I remember the police came to the market one evening because the boys had gotten caught stealing a little hot wheels car. I had to sign a paper. I couldn't tell you what it said, don't remember. I just know I thought of all things to get caught stealing. Ha, if they only knew what they had been stealing.

"No control?"

I had none and apparently mother didn't either. They had been getting away with so many things as little kids that it was a way of life, I guess. They were only about twelve and ten at this time.

When it became apparent that I was fighting a losing battle in trying to keep the market and keeping a roof over everyone's head, I humbly went to my stepbrother, Jim, and talked to him about closing his business in town and coming back to the market and working together. I think he thought about it, but that never happened. What happened was there came a day when we had to close the doors, and the building and its contents were auctioned off to pay creditors.

One of the last things I had to do was to clean out the huge freezer that had spoiled boxes of meat in it. The electricity had been shut off and it seemed with each entry into the freezer and each box that I lifted off the shelves and from the floors onto a dolly not only hurt my back but also caused me to gag and want to throw up. I had to drag the weighted down dolly through gravel and then lift and toss each box into the dumpster. I was alone and it had to be done.

The auction was held and Jim bought the market. I heard from former employees that he was lazy and didn't want to work; and therefore, he lost the market as well.

Eldon had gone to Norman, Oklahoma, where my

brother Don lived to start a new life. She left her brats with Ron and me. My sister had been driving around Vinita in our Cadillac when she was fourteen. Rat, our past employee, let her drive his car around when mother left with ours. I guess Teresa never got caught driving at such a young age.

Fred, on the other hand, did. They almost had him up on Grand Larceny charges at age ten. He said he found a car with keys in it and decided to drive it. Problem was he ran through some yard and hedges, and then buried the keys and ran. Ron got him to tell him where he hid the keys.

Also while in my care, my brothers had gotten caught shooting out street lights with BB guns by one of the schools.

So mother came to get her children before the state took them away from her. My sister stayed with us a little bit longer. I don't know when she would have come back for her kids but she just about had to after the car incident. Granted, I used to whip them and tried to discipline them, but it did no good.

CHAPTER TWELVE

Mother wasn't finished with her shenanigans, not by a long shot. She came back to Vinita a few times while Jim still had the market. She had some of the checks from the market and she used them to get money. I know she was pretty desperate. I think the only income coming in was the two social security checks for my younger brothers. I don't remember the amount but pretty sure they were under $100.00 apiece. She ended up with nothing, absolutely nothing from the market. Between the lawyer's fees, back taxes, bank note and a huge bill that Jim racked up with the meat packing company while he was running it. She did get the Cadillac, but had to sell it soon after moving to Norman in order to basically survive.

I don't remember or perhaps didn't know how she was doing it but she was taking the checks to stores as if they were payroll checks and getting them cashed. I think she was even wearing a wig at the time to disguise herself.

She made me drive her to a place called "The Buffalo Ranch." There, I know she went into the clothing store and bought a few things with a check and took the rest in cash. You know you could do things like that then with checks. I knew what she was doing was very, very bad, and I was a nervous wreck, but what could I do? Just as when I was a child, she had control over me.

As we were driving back to my house, a car with two well-dressed men sped past us and looked at me. I didn't think much of it then, but several days later after mother had gone back to Norman, an OSBI agent came to my house and explained to me about hot checks being written. I thought about those men that sped by eyeing me. They were the OSBI agents. He asked me to sign several different names on a piece of paper, and realized I had not signed any of the checks. I was in the clear, but eventually mother got caught. I assumed Jim had been covering the checks that she had been writing, but maybe he got tired of it. She got arrested for the last check she passed and spent a weekend in jail. That was it. She walked out and I never heard another thing about it. I wanted her to believe that I had pulled some strings. I think she thought I had, but never thanked me. Maybe Jim paid for that one last check and they let her go. Maybe God intervened and there was a miracle because there weren't even any records after the fact.

Anyway she went back to Norman. Eldon got a job and my mother and Don opened an Italian deli. That didn't last too long though. I suspect knowing what kind of person my brother was, he gave food away to anyone who couldn't afford it, and mother probably bought booze with profits, if any.

"Speaking of drinking, how were you doing with that? You mentioned drinking your senior year, Did it continue?"

No, I didn't drink much after that until after Ron and I were married. Then we would go out about once a week on the weekends to a place called "Bowlins." It was a family owned store, grill and club out in the boonies. We probably wouldn't have known about it except they did buy meat from the market. Also Opal, who was married to a Bowlin, worked for us and had actually become one of my close friends.

So, yes, I would drink that night at the club so I could have some fun. I was too self-conscious about everything to ever have much fun. I drank so I could have fun dancing without thinking I was being judged and maybe it gave me some temporary relief from my life. I do know that I could play the heck out of pool when intoxicated. It really made Ron mad because he wanted to be the great pool player. Sometimes he would leave me out there. He would either go home or he would fall asleep in the car waiting for me.

This wasn't a place you wanted to be left alone. It could get pretty wild at times. They always had a band playing and people came from Tulsa, Bartlesville, and even Kansas. There weren't too many white people that went there then.

"Were you worried when Ron left you there?"

No, not at all because Opal and her husband were always there, as was Rat and Walter. I knew they wouldn't let anything happen to me.

Never was much of a drinker; only when I went out dancing. I have had a few instances with pot and one time I did hashish, but never tried anything else. I faced the world sober and as firmly as I could. I don't like not being in control. A dentist gave me laughing gas once and I got hateful. I have to be in control -- I like controlling situations. I thrived at my managerial positions and loved being the boss.

"That's understandable. Did your mother stay in Norman?"

After she came and got my brothers, yes, but I remember one time she came back to Vinita and stayed a few days with Ron and me. Not sure why. For years after this visit, I believed what had transpired one night was in retaliation for Buss always wanting me.

I woke up and heard my mother and Ron talking in the living room. I got up and turned a light on and found them both lying on the couch together. I was really shocked and said some stupid thing like, "Well, ain't this a howdy doody!" They said it wasn't what it looked like -- that Ron had gotten cold as they were talking. But I knew Ron and wouldn't put it past him to try something with any woman, and I knew my mother. She would give him just enough rope to hang himself, and perhaps she wanted to hurt me.

It was never brought up until many, many years later. She told me that Eldon had caught Ron with one of his old girlfriends, and somehow he and mom were talking about it that night. She wanted to tell me but he begged her not to. Then he got cold and got under the covers with her on the couch. And some of that might be true, but my knowledge of the two of them would account for any underlying intentions on both their parts.

This incident lead me to someone else's arms, well, not

arms so much as bed. Someone I had a crush on for quite a while – so in retaliation I had sex with him. Since Ron was the only one I had ever been with, I felt really guilty. It took me a long, long time to get over that feeling. My friend, Opal, helped me through it, but it was inevitable that Ron would find out somehow. When he did he acted like a crazy man.

My sister, Teresa, and I had a fight and she threatened to tell Ron. I knew she wouldn't have, but if there was any chance, I wanted to be the one to tell him. I picked him up from work and just came out with it. He jumped out of the car when I came to a stop sign. That wasn't the first time he ever jumped out of a car, nor his last. I left him there and drove home. When he arrived home he started yelling and tearing up things in the house. He also used a little axe on the furniture. I tried to leave, but he wouldn't let me. He tore my blouse off. I put another one on and he tore that off. I guess he knew I wouldn't go out like that. I didn't see Teresa come home, but she did. She either saw or heard what was going on and called the sheriff's office.

Now when Ron and I were dating, there was this deputy sheriff who liked me. I liked him too, but he was several years older, a widower and had four children. He helped find my car one night when my mother came home drunk to the hidey house sometime after my graduation and said, "Go get your car out of hock." I couldn't imagine what that meant so I got up and rode around in a cab looking for it until midnight when they closed. I called the deputy and he found my brand new car in someone's yard blocks from our house. He also found me sleeping in my car at a park one night when I didn't want to go home, and we went for a coke.

This wasn't the first time mother rode off with my car and failed to bring it home. One time I got a call from the Highway Patrol asking me if I wanted to come and pick my mother up or they were going to have to take her to jail. Of course I didn't want her in jail, so I got a taxi to take me to the specified location. I sat high in the taxi to get sight of my car but didn't see it. I thought I was in the wrong place until I saw a wrecker. I hurried over to where it was parked and saw my new beautiful poppy orange 73

Malibu sideways in a deep ditch. She said as she made the turn the car slipped on ice and that's where she ended up. She also said the police opened the door, looked down at her and asked, "Grace, have you been drinking?" "Hell no, I'm drunk," she said she replied.

"They allowed you to take her home?"

Yes. Many people, well-to-do people, drank a lot in this town and got away with many things.

"I see. So continue with the fight you and Ron had."

Well, this deputy friend did not come to our house that day, but sent four cops to the house. They came in both doors and found me sitting on the floor trying to pick up pieces of things Ron had destroyed. They probably thought I was going to be like my mother and let this guy beat on me, etc., but I knew better. They took him outside and talked to him. A few days later this deputy sheriff came to see how I was and talked to me. Years later I heard he was into politics in some other town and doing very well. Wish I had given him a chance, but oh no, I was afraid of men and I thought I was in love with Ron. I had sex with Ron. I was a virgin until Ron. I had to be with him and then when I got pregnant, I really thought I had to be with him. Ron was young and immature and was always going to be just that. I ended up with both eyes blackened slightly that day and was stupid enough to believe I deserved it for being unfaithful.

I eventually started to not like Ron and then that eventually turned to hate.

I knew it was over when I could no longer stand to hear his voice or for him to touch me. Even though I grew to hate Ron, I gave him one last chance and he blew it. He was supposed to go to his two week National Guard Camp but instead he hitched a ride with a trucker to Florida. I don't know what he was thinking, but he ended up being shipped to Germany, active duty for a couple of years for skipping out on camp. I got a divorce.

"Did you ever allow him to hit you after that first time?"

No, but once when we were divorced and I was living in Norman, I had gone to Vinita so he and his parents could see our daughter. He was working at one of the quarter horse race tracks and I don't know what was said as we stood alone in the stalls, but he swung at me and managed to punch me right in the mouth. I was so mad I threatened to press charges, went to his parents' house, grabbed my daughter and told them I was going to press charges. They just looked at me with no response. I'm sure his mother was delighted that he popped me. Instead, I just drove back to Norman.

That's the only other time he laid a hand on me. Our five and a half year relationship was a waste of time and energy. It consisted of many immature acts and senselessness from Ron trying to be unfaithful, to Ron thinking he could take my daughter away from me even before we were married. He also ran off to some other girlfriend in Missouri the day after our daughter was born. He blamed that on his parents brainwashing him and promising him money to start over in Missouri. Our time also consisted of Ron's unwillingness to work, his mother hating me, his father wanting to get into my pants, and our wasted escape to California and back to Vinita. My mother hated Ron and his family and his mother hated us. Finally we moved to Edmond, Oklahoma, where he tried to work and I left him. That was about it. A deplorable time. I know people say the only good thing that came out of such a relationship was their son or daughter. I always told people I had my daughter by myself, no help. She was mine and only mine.

"Was that the last you saw him?"

Just about. He had come to Norman a few times when he got out of the Guard. He wanted to get back with me. I remember his first visit; I told him there was no way I would ever go back with him, he threw himself down a flight of stairs. I just slammed the door as he tumbled down fourteen steps. A few minutes later he came back into my apartment and said, "That hurt." (duh)

Another visit and things didn't go his way -- he jumped out of my car. This time it was moving. Eventually he got the message and went back to stay with mommy and daddy.

He did come to Norman again when our daughter was graduating. I really didn't want to see him and was happy that it had gotten so late that I had gone to bed. I told my daughter, "He better not bother me." They visited and he left. She told me he wanted to see me, but she warned him to not even think about it. Maybe he was just a little bit afraid of me. I remember when we were married he said he used to be afraid to go to sleep some nights if we had had a fight. He was afraid I was going to kill him in the middle of the night. I don't know where people get this stuff. (smile)

I did see him one more time many years after our divorce when I went to Vinita to visit a couple of friends. He happened to see me going into a Brahms and followed me in. I told him if he wanted to talk to me he could meet me at the American Legion later. I didn't want him to bother me while I was visiting with my sweet friend, Johnny. He was there at the Legion when I arrived and never shut his mouth. As usual he talked non stop about nothing and drove me crazy. How happy I was to have not been with him all those years.

Ron used to brag about being married to me even after we were divorced and people didn't believe him. When he was at basic training, he said he got beaten up for showing the other guys a couple pictures of me, one very provocative. He said he got beaten up another time while still at basic and they stole his watch. I remember a kid from high school punching him in the mouth at the Sonic one night when I was with him. Apparently, he had said something about the girl this guy was dating that happened to be Ron's ex-girlfriend. Ron had just the kind of mouth deserving of a good punch now and then. Seeing him at the Legion was the last time I ever saw him, but not the last time I talked to him.

"So what became of him?"

I know he married three times, had another daughter, was on disability quite early in life, came to see our daughter one more time when she was pregnant and gave her a high chair. He called both my daughter and me a few times later in life while with his third wife. He was always angry with his parents and would express how much he hated them. Then he called us when he was diagnosed with throat cancer. I was cordial to him, but he still had nothing significant to say. Somehow he was still that eighteen year old immature boy. He was sweet but not much upstairs.

His wife called when he went to the hospital once and she acted as if I was her best friend. My daughter had met her and said she was very nice, but I didn't want to be her friend. I felt sorry for her. She was afraid and I guess she felt some connection with us. He got better but you know eventually it all goes south at some point and no matter how much you think and hope that person is going to get better again, they don't. When that happened and he was back in the hospital several months later, I knew it was his time. His wife said he wanted to see us. They lived in Joplin, Missouri. My daughter didn't want to go and I sure didn't want to see him like that. I texted him a couple of pictures of the two of us when we were dating and another of us with our daughter. It was very difficult to understand him over the phone but I managed to understand that he was grateful for the pictures and that he loved us. He was 57.

His wife continued to call me after his passing. I felt really bad for her, but it was causing me great distress. I finally had to send her a card expressing how sorry I was for her but there was a reason I left Ron and I didn't want to think about him or his family. I asked her if she had any friends or family close or perhaps she should seek some counseling. The last time we talked she seemed better and had indeed gone to some counseling. About a year later I tried to call her just to see how she was doing, but her phones had been disconnected.

Even though Buss tried to "get me," my term for what his ultimate goal might have been, I managed to stay a virgin until I was nineteen, and then it was with Ron --my first mistake when it came to men. But then you have to understand, I was basically afraid of guys, after all, mother was going to break both of my legs if I got pregnant, even though I had no idea how to get pregnant. I had a step-father that wanted to touch me, rub up against me all the time and wanted to have sex with me. I knew the touching was wrong as a child, just didn't know what it could have led to and then again, remember I couldn't even remember what had happened to me that night when he followed me upstairs to the bedroom, pushed me onto the bed and started to come down on me as I put my knees up to stop him. No recollection of what happened next.

So I got involved with Ron because I was not afraid of him. I liked boys a lot, especially if they were cute, and at that time Ron was cute. Immature and not too bright, but cute, and he was not an "Okie." I swore I would never be with an Okie. I still thought I was a New Yorker and better than an Okie. I had to have more or something different. Yes, I think different is what I wanted most definitely.

So I moved to Norman to be near my family and to get a divorce from Ron. That mission accomplished; I got a job, put my daughter in daycare, and soon got my own apartment before I started feeling comfortable enough to begin a new phase of my life. I was a single mom living in Norman, Oklahoma -- college town and home of the famous Sooners. At that time in the middle 70's, the college was full of foreign students mainly from Latin America, Asia, and the Middle East.

I wasn't interested in any Asian's, but was very attracted to dark eyes, hair and skin, and a fan of great romance stories in the desert.

The first young man to catch my eye looked like Omar Sharif. Those big brown, half sad eyes were to die for. His full dark, somewhat curly hair outlined his beautiful light brown, perfect cute face. This came about when I was working in a convenience store. Two young men came in and started to talk to me and flirt a little. In his strong Persian accent but pretty good English, one asked, "If you would go out with one of us, who would it be, me or him?" "Who would you pick?" I should have picked the one asking the question. He married an American and became a very successful businessman. My short lived affair with the other actually ended up with heartbreak when I found out he was married to an American girl and was just cheating on her. Of course, I would not see him anymore when I found this out. My

Omar had a younger brother and the other guy had an older brother that would be coming to America soon. They asked me if I would meet the older brother. Sure, I didn't mind. I thought in the back of my mind that it might make Omar jealous.

Actually, this older brother treated me very good. He took me out and we actually went to my first concert -- The Commodores. I was a bit shocked when I saw a body being stretchered out before the concert even started. I heard they OD'ed. He and I dated for a few months and I think he was very fond of me. I liked him but didn't have feelings for him. He wasn't bad looking but not cute and not really my type -- you know, he was too nice. My sister had been seeing the younger boy. I was under the impression they were friendly, but had had sex. In any event I knew they were not serious which led me to not care about the affair I had with the young boy.

The one I was seeing had gone back home to Iran for a visit. The young boy came over to my house one day. He was tall unlike his brother Omar, but equally cute. Not as cute but cute in a different way. He could hardly speak any English. He got a large knife from my kitchen and with a huge smile on his face that was not frightening and with some giggling; he forced me into the bedroom asking for sex. I knew I could stop him at any time from forcing me. He was not threatening even though he was taller than I and stronger; he was playing and I liked it. This was the beginning of our little affair. His body was perfect. The sex was exceptional, hot, sweaty, unadulterated and lasted for hours each time. He was about seventeen; I was twenty four.

The other came back from Iran about a week after my first encounter with the boy. He was a little sad but apparently respected what was going on because we never slept together again. My affair with the boy lasted a long time. Maybe close to a year. I don't remember how or why it ended. Perhaps he left Oklahoma.

Over the years I had seen my Omar a few times at a club, in a grocery store and even at a restaurant or two with his wife – his American wife, who he was married to when he was having sex with me. I asked him once about his little brother. He told me he lived in California and owned a string of gas stations. I didn't say anything about how finding out he was married hurt me or asked how he was doing. I didn't care any longer. He got older, turned premature grey, got shorter and was not so cute anymore. I just couldn't understand why I kept seeing him around off and on. He didn't even live in the same town. Maybe just so my past could haunt me.

CHAPTER THIRTEEN

Perhaps it was my promiscuous behavior that brought the devil into my daughter's and my life. One of the hardest things to accept in life is not being able to protect your children. As much as you try, you can and probably will fail. I did and it is still so hard for me to accept. It's one of those things I stuff deep down whenever I am reminded of my failure in this area.

My daughter was around four. I, being the bad mother that I was, seeing my young Iranian and going out partying on the weekends, I let my brothers babysit occasionally. I allowed Fred to watch her once without Mark and apparently he attempted to do sexual things with her. He was eleven at the time. I was not gone very long because I still took him home that night. I sensed something was wrong. I remember asking my daughter questions and since we had a wonderful mother, daughter relationship, she told me what he had done. I didn't have to beat it out of her like my mother did me. She knew she could tell me anything even at that young age. I couldn't believe the one thing I especially wanted to protect her from had happened.

"So you're speaking metaphorically about the devil? And what did you do?"

Not metaphorically. No. And what I did first was put my precious daughter to bed and I began to drink. I was so enraged. The things that went through my mind were flashbacks of my childhood and his father touching me, and then this little bastard touched my daughter. My daughter! Then I thought of my mother and the hell she put me through always leaving me with Buss and then giving me the third degree about whatever may have happened -- literally slapping it out of me. Then I felt guilt for leaving my daughter with him.

So I fell asleep or probably passed out and awoke at three a.m. wanting to kill him. I didn't need to get dressed. I gently woke my daughter and wrapped her in a blanket and let her lie down in the back seat. I drove to my mother's house, walked in quietly and found Fred asleep. I started to strangle him, which of course woke him. I remember somehow pulling him out of the bed by his neck and he followed. I took him outside and began to beat his ass.

There was a storage shed in the yard with part of the tin siding broken. I wanted to and had visions of taking him over there, lifting him over my head and slamming him onto the tin, cutting him in half.

That's what I wanted to do, even though it was probably impossible. Then I thought of Mother again and how it was all her fault.

I dragged his ass into the house, into her bedroom and I threw him onto the bed, onto her, and I said, "Here's the product of your love for Bussie!"

She got up and was telling me to get out of their house, yelling is more like it. I had intended to leave but she kept following me and telling me to get out. I turned to her and slapped her right across the face -- hard, and then I left.

"Oh my. Where was your daughter?"

She was still asleep in the car. She never knew a thing. I don't really remember driving home. After that, I had nothing to do with any of my family for a very long time. I have a friend, Toine, who worked for the Department of Human Services (DHS). I met her when she came to my house when I needed help from DHS to pay for daycare for my daughter while I worked. I didn't want help, but needed it at the time. I didn't want financial aid or food stamps, just daycare help, and I didn't want them all up in my business. This was the attitude she faced the day she came to my house. She probably thought I was somewhat of a bitch as some people thought upon first impressions, so I heard, but I soon felt a connection with this woman and liked her almost immediately.

We soon became very good friends. Our children played together and we spent many hours of family-like time with she and her children. It was a good for us. I felt Toine was very wise and understanding, and I looked up to her a lot. I told her what had happened and she advised me to report the incident. At first I was afraid of what might happen to Fred and, believe it or not, I didn't want to put my mother through anything. The more I thought about it though, the more I felt hate for Mother and Fred. Also, it was my duty to protect my child or another child, and I felt my mother deserved whatever comes her way. She did not protect me or stand up for me, but by God, I was going to for my daughter.

"So you turned him in?"

Yes, they both, Mother and Fred had to go in front of a judge and were ordered to go to counseling.

"Good for you. Are you going to tell about the devil?"

Oh yes, the devil. Well, like I said, I didn't have anything to do with the family for quite a while. They would call or try to come by, but I wouldn't answer the door or I was forced to slam the door in their faces, especially my mother's. I recall her saying I had become very, very hateful.

Anyway, it was during this time of hatefulness and bitterness that I fell asleep one night and experienced a dream, but not like a dream. My body locked up including my jaw. I was lying on my back and, within me, was expecting something. A door appeared at the bottom of my bed to the right. It looked like a nice normal door with a little light coming from underneath. I couldn't move but my head was tilted in that direction. So I waited for whatever I felt like I was expecting.

Soon the devil appeared at the bottom of my bed. Directly in the middle -- directly in front of me. It was tall, had a jagged like, huge head. It lightly glowed from the inside out. The color was an ugly green. I can now tell you that it looked like the color of the green slime they pour on kids on those kid shows -- only a little darker. Maybe with a tint of blue mixed in.

"Oh, my God!"

Exactly what I did, I called for Jesus. My body still locked including my jaw, but through my clenched teeth I called out. "Jesus, Jesus, Jesus." After a moment something started whispering into my left ear. I could feel it's breath on my ear and hear its beautiful voice, but couldn't tell you what it said. I don't know if it was Christ or an angel. I do know that it seemed like it talked to me for a long time. Eventually my body started to loosen up. Satan, by that time, had lifted his arm up as in reaching out for me and expecting me to go with him. As my body was released from his bondage, his arm dropped as in disgust and another door appeared to the left. This door looked like an old castle door with ugly vines all over it. Satan disappeared through the door, I assume.

"Then what happened?"

Well, then what happened was, well before that, I had taken my little girl in to get checked for physical and emotional stress -- positive reports on both accounts and relief on my part. I, on the other hand, ended up going to therapy for about a year. I wasn't accustomed to talking about my feelings. That was never allowed. My mother never let me talk or explain anything, and I never had anyone that I could talk to. For several sessions I couldn't speak. I was unable to talk with the counselor and she was very understanding. I could only write what I felt. She accepted this method until I was able to talk. Funny thing, now that I think of her, she reminded me of Mrs. Parkhurst, the psych teacher and counselor I didn't care for in high school.

Finally, I got nicer and at some time the family became part of our lives again to continue in the dysfunctional manner that we were accustomed to, and to continue with my co-dependent lifestyle with and for them. I never left my daughter with my brothers again.

I told my brother, Don, about my supernatural experience. He had quit going to the Catholic Church a long time before this happened and simply looked at it from a Christian's point of view. He also had talked with some of his Christian friends. He said, which I believe, that I was at such a low point in my life at that time that the devil thought he could get me. I truly believe calling out to Christ saved me that night from whatever evil could have been in store for me and my life from then on. Thank God that my faith has always been strong. Had I not called for Christ and reached out to Satan, who knows, I could have been an entirely different person.

Years later I told Father Caligiuri of my experience, but he didn't have the same view as my brother and his friends. He more or less said it was a dream. I got mad and didn't discuss it further with him. I often wonder why the Catholic religion is so quick to discard the supernatural world leaking into our realm which they know does. And publically, although they are the ones performing most of the exorcisms, will just blow off such events. They know a lot more than they expose.

I will say that Satan knows exactly what to use to get you and to make a person do evil, terrible things, and fill them with hate. He will use the one thing that you swore wouldn't come into your life again or just not happen to you at all. He will use that as often as he can to try to break you and your faith or bond with the Lord, your savior. My savior.

I didn't become an angel after this. I still took care of my daughter and myself. I continued to go out drinking and dancing and occasionally had a one night stand. I didn't want to get involved with anyone nor did they. It was college guys wanting to party and have sex, and that's all I thought I wanted too. Deep down I probably just wanted someone to love me though.

My sister was going with a college student from Panama who eventually did become her husband, and they had a son. So I began hanging around the Panamanians, Columbians, Nicaraguans, Venezuelans. Latin Lovers; ha. They were some of the worse lovers I'd ever had. Although there was one Venezuelan who was pretty good. We, too, lasted for hours and he was very romantic. I remember many nights in front of his fireplace with pretty glasses full of wine. He actually started to fall in love with me, but I couldn't see me with him. He, too, became very successful I heard in the garment business.

"It seemed like you were pushing away the ones that were most interested in you."

And I knew I was, but I didn't know why. I guess I didn't feel worthy of love or perhaps I didn't think it was possible. I also wanted things to be my way because I had been hurt several times. I remember a Nicaraguan college boy whose father was some diplomat in their country. I didn't have sex with him. He wanted me to rub his back and I thought, F*** this, who the hell is he for me to rub his back. He thought he was going to get it all that night. I left, not caring that he was a friend of my soon to be brother-in-law. There were a few others that don't need mentioning and I soon moved on back to my Middle Eastern men.

I had a few one night stands during the next few years of my life. I didn't care. It was all about sex. I was getting what I wanted. I didn't care about any of them. I did, however, spend some time with another young man who was attending college. He was more than a one night stand, a cute Egyptian pilot. I can see his picture in my head with a pilot's cap on. He was very sweet. He had very dark skin with big beautiful lips. I remember sitting on the floor in a circle with other young Arab men eating breakfast from a large bowl in the middle of the floor. Arabic style, where the flat bread is under the meal, and you break some of the bread and scoop the food up with the bread and eat. No silverware. This affair was short lived. Don't remember how it ended either. I think I just kept walking away and not looking back. I wonder sometimes if they remember me. They are all old men now. I bet they do think of me once in a while. It's only natural. What a free and wild time in my life.

CHAPTER FOURTEEN

Being with the Middle Eastern men prompted me to write my second screenplay, "Khayal" (a fairy tale). It is a story about college students, of course. The girl is a ballerina who meets a young man from the Middle East, later to find out he is a prince. He has to suddenly go home and leaves America. She finds out she is pregnant, but lets him leave without telling him. She has the baby, continues with her career of becoming a great dancer, and performs several years later at the White House where he is a guest. He realizes who she is and wants to see her. Of course he sees his son and knows instantly that its his. They renew their love and she travels to his country, which is in turmoil. She gets captured, he saves her, etc., but I think I killed the child off and she ends up in an institution. I could always dig it out of my file cabinet and change the ending.

Perhaps I thought at the time that this kind of relationship could never work, so in order to end their relationship, I had to take the boy or I thought if it didn't work out, then the prince would take the boy from his mother and she couldn't bear that.

"Sounds interesting."

I continued to work and write and raise my daughter all the while dealing with my mother, her alcoholism, her wild children, their financial woes. I had a full plate all the time.

I met a couple of young men from Nigeria. Not on the same night, but soon one after the other. I didn't know at the time but they were friends. Here again, I had to have different men, of course. Nice gentlemen always. One was an architect student at the University, the other, I didn't know what he was studying, but he became a state worker in the child welfare department.

"Did you have relationships with these men?"

Yes. But they also seemed like friends. You also can see that all of the young men were not just average. I like to think that they were all of a higher class of people. They all became successful. So I was not just sleeping with anyone. I was picky, believe it or not, and they all treated me with respect -- always. These, too, were short lived; and I had come across one of them over the years a couple of times in a grocery store or at a musical event in Norman. I tried to avoid him because I was with another person and was afraid of what he might say to me in front of who I was with.

But what does it really matter? Black, white, brown. I know we are all human, all God's children. What matters most is that I was a sinner. A terrible sinner. These were not my worst sins, but some pretty bad sinning was going on. I was going through whatever it was that I was going through and pretty much didn't care to analyze. It may have been acts of revenge in some way. All I know is that I was free from anyone's discipline or criticisms. Maybe it was rebellion. I have no idea. I was just...just.

"No judgment being made here."

Some months after meeting these two Nigerians, my sister, my daughter and I were at a Taco Tico restaurant in Norman. I noticed a couple of Middle Eastern men seated at a table. One was eating, the other not. For some reason I was interested in the one that was not eating. I don't know if I thought he was good looking. I don't know if it was the fact that he wasn't eating anything. I have no idea what it was about him that drew my attention to him to a most interesting degree.

Now this was the time when Iran was going through their revolution. I had a bumper sticker sprawled across my bright red pinto and it read, "Khomeini kiss my gas." I believe it had something to do with the Ayatollah Khomeini revealing that his country had enough oil, etc., that his country should not have to pay for it, and was against the Shah selling it to other countries. Maybe it was our statement that we didn't need their oil.

We had finished our meal and headed out the door. I had this weird feeling that they were going to try to talk to us. I didn't see them look at us or anything I just had this weird feeling.

I knew they were Iranians. I knew which were Arabs, Iranians, Pakistani, Indian, etc.

"By their looks?"

Their looks, their color, their accents. I had also noticed that Iranians were more apt to have nice butts and the Arabs not so much. Arabs seemed to be flat. Also Arabs seemed to drag their feet when wearing sandals. At least these were the things I had noticed.

We got closer to the car and since I knew instinctively what was going to happen, I quickly ripped the sticker off. We got into the car and I started to drive out of the parking lot. Just as I got to the end of the lot and just before I was to pull out into the street here they came. They pulled up right beside us and said, "hi" and something else I am sure before asking for our phone numbers.

We gave them my number. At the time, my sister was married. She was eighteen, I was twenty six. I got a call one night from one of them, the one that wasn't eating – the one I was interested in the minute I saw him that day at the fast food restaurant. We started talking and we talked for some time. At some point in the conversation he asked about my sister. I informed him that she was married and had a little one. We continued to talk and years later, he revealed that the day they saw us, he was interested in my sister. I am so happy, but not really, to have taken that punishment from her.

"Punishment?"

I say punishment because that's what I get for being a stupid whore.

"Not a whore. A young woman going through a lot of things. Things you could never understand."

Well, so I started to see this man, David. A Jewish Iranian at that. Jewish, mind you. A persecuted religion in Iran. David said it wasn't too bad for the Jews when it was ruled by the Shah, who was ousted by an Iranian Revolution in 1979. The Shah was supported by the U.S. and the U.K., which Iranians perceived the Shah as a puppet of non-Muslim western power. When I met David it was the time very close to the ousting of the Shah.

"So you were very interested in this man."

Yes, but I wasn't through partying and dancing. I was still occasionally seeing the two Nigerians, but was slowly letting them go by this time, and had never let David know that I was this kind of person. I even hooked up once with an OU basketball player, whose name I never got nor even cared to. I was like a man in a woman's body. He wanted to see me again but I just told him, "I know where you live" as I quietly shut the door. I had these men and didn't care to see them again once I was done with them. Never wanting to get involved with any of them until David.

Men were always attracted to me. I didn't know why but they were. I didn't even care for the species and if I thought I was getting something from them, I really wasn't. What was it really all for? Why was I doing this? At this point it doesn't matter. I was what I was. It was what it was. People had come into my life and I released them. People passing through this life perhaps left with just a fleeting thought now and then about your encounter with them and they with you. Makes life interesting at least.

"Has certainly made yours interesting."

I got to a point where I was sort of seeing David. He was unattainable though which is what a stupid girl craves. So I needed to conquer him. Had to have him. Just as I had to have Ron. Why, when there were others who wanted me? No, I had to have what I wanted and if other men wanted a relationship, I was out of there fast.

So I thought my days of meeting other men were over until one night when I was out again at a club, I met a couple of men. They came and sat with me, introduced themselves. One was from India; I believe the other said, "Hello, I am Mario." Mario, I thought, yeah right. Most of the foreign students had made up names. Mostly they used American names. He said he was from

Italy but I knew by his accent he was Arab. So we talked and talked the night away. He was very charming and sweet. I liked him. Of course later on; not that night, he revealed that he was from Libya. He said he had some Italian blood in him and he was an engineering student. Mario was not his real name but I will continue to use it as I did then.

Mario was everything that David wasn't. He was romantic, sweet and sensitive. David and I weren't serious and so I began to see Mario when I could.

Now previously there were a couple of foreigners that had asked me to marry them in order for them to stay in the U.S. I didn't really consider it. Well maybe briefly, but when David asked me, my thoughts were, "I think I love this man, I have to have him and if I would do this for anyone it would be the Jewish guy, not the Muslim, right?" I had nothing against Muslims. I had met several and was friends with them and not just men -- whole families. Did not have a problem with the Muslims I had met. Dear, dear people. Perhaps I was trying to find favor with God. Also I had to consider who I was bringing into my daughter's life. I didn't trust any man, but seemed to feel some trust with David. David said I didn't have to marry him in order for him to stay in the U.S. "I could pay a lawyer two thousand dollars," I remember him saying with his strong accent. Maybe this was what I was supposed to do, save the Jewish man, and long term thought was to get him to believe in Jesus. Probably easier than my mother trying to get an atheist to believe in Christ, right?

"Maybe."

The day of our marriage was very stressful. My family didn't know what I had planned on doing. My friend, Toine, knew and Wilma from Vinita was in Norman to visit her daughter and my mother. She came to my house that morning to stay with my daughter who was about four and a half. She was my mother's friend also, but she never told my mother. No one discouraged me really. But I probably would have gone through with it anyway. I think Toine might have said something like she hoped I knew what I was doing. I had told my best friend, Vinnie. She did not like the idea. She didn't think it was a good idea to marry someone for that reason; so he could stay here and get a green card. She didn't know I was falling in love with him. Later in life she said she couldn't remember if I said I loved him or not at that time. I responded with, "Of course I did," because when it came to men I could only love the wrong ones! She thought it had something to do with security. The only security I remember was that he seemed to want to protect me from my family. He didn't want them to come over to the house. What I took for trying to protect me from the stress of the family might have mostly been trying to possess me -- kind of like the evil stepfather, Buss.

I drove to his apartment. David, I and several of his friends drove to Oklahoma City to the courthouse. I was dressed in a nice beige skirt and jacket. The men, all Persian, were dressed in suits. We had to walk a ways to the court house. My stomach was full of butterflies and in knots. David was nervous as hell, I could tell. He walked ahead of the rest of us and I was encircled by four men in their suits. People passing by looked at us strangely. They probably wondered who is this strawberry blonde American girl and why does she look like she is being protected. Or better yet, maybe they thought who is this prisoner of these foreigners?

It was June; it was hot. We arrived in the courthouse and there were several couples waiting to get married. I had seen something like this on TV shows but never witnessed in person. We filed in and were married by the Justice of the Peace surrounded by a handful of other couples. Signed, sealed; not delivered, but the deed was done.

It dawned on me that both my marriages started out a secret, but then I was accustomed to many secrets so just shrugged it off.

We left the building walking in the same manner as before. We walked into a large bank. I didn't know why. David still hadn't really said anything to me all this time. It was very, very strange but I was still going along with the whole ordeal. One of David's friends answered my question. One of them needed to talk to the banker, something about getting a loan or paying on a loan, something about his Persian rug import business.

We sat. We waited. I could feel interested eyes on me from the tellers and customers. I was still extremely stressed, wondering how all this would play out. The plan was to be married for a few months and "Get divorce," as David said. "Get divorce." I probably didn't want to "Get divorce," and I also didn't want to get into any kind of trouble with immigration. But really, I felt like I was doing a good thing. I was falling in love with him. Not sure why but I was. Oh that's right; I could only do that with the wrong men. Not the men that liked me or wanted me.

I did have a couple of American boys that wanted me to marry them. I had some nice American men that wanted to date me. Hell, I even had a boss that tried to get me to go out with him many times. He was a commercial pilot, but he and the others were just too nice. I couldn't have a nice guy. I didn't feel right with a nice guy. This boss even offered me a thousand dollars to sleep with him once. I rode around with him in his sporty convertible and we went to an OU Basketball game once, but I never slept with him. I was not attracted to him. He was blonde. I was, however, attracted to his friend who was also my other boss at the convenience store. He was married though and had children. I would never knowingly sleep with or get involved with a married man.

One night this other boss did come to my house. It was almost midnight. These two friends owned a convenience store just a few doors from my duplex. I managed the store. I opened the door. I could tell he had been drinking. He was bringing me the cash bag so I could open the next morning. Totally unexpected. He could have hidden it in the building. I don't recall him ever bringing me the money to open with. Maybe it was a special occasion that I had to open that next day or maybe it was just an excuse to come over. Apparently he had been attracted to me also for some time.

It was pouring down rain and there was only a small easement just above the door so he was getting wet. I opened the door wide. He stood for a second before coming in as he said, "I brought the money bag over." I said something about it pouring and he should come in out of the rain. The next thing I can recall now is that we were on the couch kissing. The attraction had finally gotten the best of both of us. It was getting extremely hot and heavy and close to where we would strip and just do it, but I stopped it cold. I was proud of myself for having the control, but also there was no way I could do this and face his wife and kids. I liked his wife. Even if I hadn't liked her, I couldn't do that to another woman. I wouldn't want it done to me; I wouldn't do it to another.

 He reluctantly left, but I know that he was glad we never had sex. I could only imagine how long a secret affair with him might have gone on. I could imagine how I could lose my job and he could lose his wife and children. This way, the next day when his wife came into the store and asked me if her husband had come over to my house last night, and she did, I was able to say, looking at her face that he had. "He brought the money bag over." She said she was worried last night because it was raining so hard and he was late getting home. I told her I was worried for him too last night and was hoping he would get home safely because of the rain. She asked me about what time he had stopped by and I think I told her around midnight. That was that. Years later when I worked for the University I ran into his wife and could still look her in the face. They were still married. I met him once for lunch many, many years after the incident. He was quite an old man then in my opinion. He was working for a law firm and I had some questions to ask and he wanted to meet for lunch. We didn't really talk about the incident much, just that we were in a way glad we didn't do anything that rainy night.

 When David and I arrived back at his apartment I was not feeling very well after the whole marriage deal. We took a nap. A nap. No sex. We laid there as strangers in our own thoughts. I can't even remember if we ate dinner. When I awoke, I went home. No honeymoon. I went home, had a few drinks and started to freak out by myself. I didn't normally drink at home. I am sure it was just a beer or two. With my daughter asleep I called my friend, Toine. She was concerned for me of course, and we talked for quite some time. She even volunteered to come over but I told her I'd be all right, but I wasn't and I wasn't for quite a while. I was kind of freaking out. I felt on edge for weeks.

We had to go to the immigration office for questioning and paperwork. We were taken into separate rooms. David had done the necessary things such as setting up a bank account with both our names. I was asked questions such as "Do you have a joint bank account?" "What is your address?" Gave them his. "What color is his toothbrush?" Something about what his favorite food is and who cooks and things like that. Luckily I was falling in love with him and the answers and the conversation flowed easily. I wasn't sure how David was doing in the next room because surely at that time he was not in love with me. In the end all went well.

I did remain living at my house for a few months. I was still friends with the Nigerians. One had loaned me seventy five dollars once and I was determined to pay him back. I didn't like to owe anyone anything. Although I didn't see them, I may have talked to them on the phone occasionally. This house was a rental and the owners wanted to sell so I had to move. I called my friend and offered him a chair that he liked a lot for my repayment of my loan. He said I didn't owe him anything, but I insisted and he finally agreed to take the chair.

My daughter and I moved to an apartment. I was still seeing Mario, because this was not a marriage made in heaven and it didn't look as if David wanted it to be real anyway. I would see Mario when I could. So now I was married to a Jewish Iranian and having an affair with, I believe, an Arab Muslim although I never asked Mario his religion.

"Oh my."

David and I continued to live separately seeing each other only on the weekends when my daughter and I would stay at his apartment. I don't know how I did it all. My daughter was in kindergarten by now and I was working at an import export business. When didn't I work? Felt as though I had worked forever. I had all my motherly duties and somehow still helped my mother financially and whatever help she may have needed. She was still with Eldon and still drank. He drank too, but he favored pot. They had fights and it seemed like the boys got into some trouble now and then. I don't know why but it seemed like I was always taking Mother to the grocery store and liquor store. I know for the most part she hid her drinking from Eldon as she did with Buss, probably because she was a mean drunk and they didn't like it.

There was a short period of time that I had attended a few Metaphysic classes because a friend from work was teaching them. I was somewhat inquisitive about dreams, always had been. My mother could never understand how my dreams were always in color and how I could remember them. I couldn't understand how she didn't dream in color or how she couldn't ever remember her dreams.

I had a dream during the time of attending these classes. Sean Connery was some kind of wizard, dressed in a silky, bright, wizardry costume including a large pointy hat.

"Sean Connery? Old Sean Connery or younger?"

Many of my dreams consist of famous actors. I would say, middle age, Connery. He was being projected onto this huge screen in a very large, gothic, futuristic kind of auditorium. As I walked closer to the screen, Sean was holding in the palm of his hand a spinning piece of metal and he was explaining that we and everything was made of energy.

In the book, "The Celestine Prophecy," it spoke of energy in everything. I actually enjoyed the classes and learned how to meditate. I enjoyed exploring my mind and experiencing creative abilities. I quit going because my strict Catholic upbringing had me feeling that it was very wrong.

Later on in life I came to believe that Christ was in perfect harmony with the universe and therefore was able to perform miracles. And the Bible states we should all be able to perform such feats. I believe if we could expand our minds as I was being shown in those classes, perhaps we could get in harmony with the universe. So was it wrong?

I had a thought one night. What if our dreams were not

just our subconscious working out the problems of the day? What if dreams were also, at times, actually remembering our past lives or even into our future? And what if, when we go to bed at night with a dilemma or problem to work out whether we remember the dream or not, we may have, that night, actually drawn from past experience and come up with a solution. I had mentioned the part about dreams being part of our future to Vinnie and she replied, "Interesting, but you'd have a hard time proving it."

CHAPTER FIFTEEN

November 1979, fifty two American diplomats were captured and held hostage by Iranian Students in Iran. Everyone that looked Middle Eastern here in the states was in danger. David worked a late shift at a Holiday Inn as a kitchen manager because he was still in college. He came over to my apartment one night after midnight. He and his friends were run off the road after work and beaten up pretty badly. I know he just wanted some comfort and he received it from me. I am quite sure he didn't stay all night because he never did stay at my place -- it was always we staying at his place. He ended up with broken ribs. The stressful situation went on for quite a while because the diplomats were held for 444 days.

It seems like it wasn't very long after this incident we were living at his apartment as it should have been. The import export place I was working at went out of business, and he may have taken us in mainly because I was temporarily unemployed. But not for long as I soon started working at a copy shop. He expected me to pay half the rent and pay for some groceries. I also provided anything my daughter needed.

When I got the job at this copy place I was giving my information to a girl who without turning around to look at me was typing the information. She asked my name and when she heard my last name she asked if I was married to a Don Landy. I told her he was my brother. Thus began our friendship. Paula knew my brother years before I had arrived in Norman. They somehow had become friends and used to hang out at the local radio station when he deejayed. Paula and I became lifelong friends after that, as did her sisters, Leslie and Cindy and I. I had always been careful in choosing friends; they were from a good family and I liked them all almost immediately.

I also met a woman named Sheila who became a very good friend. She and her husband, Bob, were two of the most generous people I had ever met. Throughout the years they were always there for my daughter and I. I don't care what it was, whether I needed to borrow some money or move some furniture, they were there. They fed us many times and even let me stay with them for several weeks later in life when I was between jobs and homes. They, especially Sheila, were always there to give me advice if I or even if I didn't want it. When Bob passed away, not only did I go view him at the funeral home, something I didn't do (view dead bodies), I didn't want to leave him. When I went to see Sheila immediately after, I cried hard. I couldn't understand my reaction to Bob dying, but Sheila said he was somewhat like a father to me. Then I understood.

Now the owners of this copy shop were an older couple and bickered back and forth at each other quite often. It was a very stressful place to work for everyone. At some point when I couldn't take it anymore and when I felt confident with my position, I actually brought up the subject during a meeting with everyone present. I explained how their behavior caused we the employees great stress, and it also made the customers uncomfortable. It was extra stressful for me because it was just like when I was a teen working in the market with Mother and Buss. I think they took it to heart and tried awfully hard to curb taking their frustrations out on each other.

CHAPTER SIXTEEN

Living with David was pretty interesting. First, I must mention that it is a custom for Jewish couples to sleep separately and not engage in sex when the woman is on her period. At first it hurt my feelings because I was in love with this man and wanted to just sleep with him. I took it as rejection and I do not like rejection. Sometimes he would even sleep on the floor. At least he gave me the bed or most times I slept with my daughter. I couldn't believe it. "What did they used to do with the women, throw them in the dungeon when they were on their periods?" I once asked.

We lived in an apartment complex where there were many other foreign students with families. There was an Iraqi couple that had five children. The husband could speak some English but the wife, hardly a word. Their children, however, could speak some English and attended the same school as my daughter. Many times I gave them a ride to school. The children always smelled dirty and never looked too clean either.

David said that in some Middle Eastern countries it's not customary to bathe every day and some men think it is manlier that they don't. He also stated that usually they were people from the villages. One year these Iraqi children were fascinated with our Christmas tree. My daughter loved the silver tree every year, and so that is the one I would put up until she finally (and I was grateful) got sick of. It was one of those that you are supposed to have a rotating colored light machine in front of it so that the tree would change colors. Well, I didn't have the light fixture. We decorated it with red velvety bulbs, red being my favorite color, and we hung icicles on it and garland also as if it were a green tree. Think we used colored lights also. We enjoyed it. The Iraqi children's eyes would light up when they came over to visit.

I had these small, hand carved wooden balancing birds setting in the seat beside me when I went to the local Walmart store, where in the parking lot there were Christmas trees for sale. I wanted to find a tree for these Iraqi kids. I didn't want to spend a lot of money nor did I have much to spend anyway. My daughter and I got out of the car and started to look around. A man came over and asked to help us. I explained my desire to get a tree for these Iraqi children. He had the kindest face, very good looking and I would say in his middle thirties. We all looked around for a bit and then with a kind smile on his face he brought over a tree for us. It reminded me a little of that Christmas tree in one of those Charlie Brown Christmas Shows. It was not very beautiful. In fact the limbs and needles were somewhat scarce and it was about four feet tall. I loved it at first sight. He gave it to me for nothing. He loaded it. I thanked him and got in the car. He came to the window and I thanked him again. I gave him the little box containing the balancing birds that I loved so much. He thanked me and kissed me on the cheek and said, "Merry Christmas." That is what Christmas is about. What a joyful experience we shared. Never saw this man again. Don't know who he was, but think of him almost every Christmas and the special encounter we shared.

Needless to say, the family accepted the tree and the decorations we gave them from our own stash. My daughter and I also made them a basket with lots of goodies in it and helped them decorate the tree. Even though they may have been Muslim, I hope they think of us once in a while especially at Christmas.

Even though David was Jewish and did his Jewish thing with the Menorah etc., he still let us have our Christmas as well as gift exchanging. This is the one time that I remember David spending a good amount of money on any gift he would get me. I have a very nice gold necklace and earrings to this day from him, and I still have a beautiful black antique gold diamond ring that I picked out for my wedding ring. I even still have the jewelry box he got me one year that plays our song, the love theme from Dr. Zhivago.

I had not received very many gifts in my life so I have

always cherished the ones I did get. I have a very nice brass lamp that my mother gave me one year for my birthday and a large painting of the ocean splashing into some rocks. I thought it was very nice of her. She actually asked a local artist to paint it knowing I loved the ocean.

Also in the beginning while living with David, I remember many of his friends coming over. There was plenty of good Persian food, dancing and drinking. I learned to dance as a Persian, eat their food and celebrate with them. He had a roommate when we met, and he lived with David for a while even after my daughter and I moved in. And there was another occasion that we had another friend living with us for a while. Because of these roommates there were parties even when David was at work. Sometimes his friends were still there when he got home after midnight. Then they would play cards all night. There was always cooking, eating and partying at our apartment.

"What did your mother think of David? I'm sure you told her at some point that you two were married."

Yes, I just don't remember how or when I told her we were married. I think she liked David at first, then not, and then liked him again. I know there was a time when we lived with him that she made some accusation concerning he and my daughter. I, of course, hated her for even suggesting such a thing. After all, how could she even bring up such a thing? I knew she had to be wrong. I tried to be so careful in picking someone and I looked for it constantly. Her accusations had to be the devil at work, I thought.

David was very strict with my daughter, but I was raised that way, and he was raised that way. I thought it was a good thing to an extent. He was a bit strict with me also. He expected me to be home when he got there. He expected a clean house and usually dinner. When he cooked it was mostly Persian dishes for which we acquired a taste for almost immediately. I really preferred Persian rather than Arabic or Indian food. Arab food seemed harsh where Persian food flavorful and just very delicious.

One night several of us went out clubbing and then to a

Persian restaurant that was actually closing up, but they let us in because there were so many of us. I am not even sure if David was with us that night or not. I was pretty drunk and remember getting up onto a table, asking them to clink their glasses in rhythm to my attempt at some pretty good Persian dancing. I can see their faces still, most of them men, looking up at me, clinking their glasses with silverware with big smiles on their faces and laughing too. I bet I was a sight. I have to admit, although David thought I was fat and said, "You should put yourself in the closet and not eat until you lose weight," I was shaped nicely. I may have been overweight some, but my stomach was small and my hips and breasts were big.

It wasn't often I wore a dress but there was this one time at one of his friend's weddings that I wore a very pretty flowery, light green dress that buttoned all the way down the front. I felt like I looked like Sophia Loren in this dress and I acted like it too that night. Sometimes girls just gotta feel pretty and good about themselves. I think David worked late that night also, but I stayed up with the dress on so he could see me in it. His reaction must have been uneventful or I would have remembered if he would had said something nice or positive.

That's how he kept me. He didn't compliment me. He didn't think I was pretty like other men did. And yet he wanted to keep me. Just as my relationship with my mother. She didn't love me, he didn't love me. Why did I keep trying to get these people to love me? I don't sing because she told me as a child that I couldn't carry a tune and David thought I was fat.

"Oh my! Was he abusive?"

Verbally and psychologically, yes, but not for quite a while after we were married. He roughed me up once and pinned me down onto the floor; he said I looked at him like I wanted to kill him. Well, I probably did then. He would threaten me with the scissors when I couldn't cut his hair right. One, I was afraid to mess it up; two, it was tight and curly; and three, I was not a barber. I would think, "Pay a couple of bucks to a barber, you cheap bastard." There was also one time that he asked me "You wanna me to take all your clothes off and make you stand in the corner?" "Well no," I said. I can't remember what I had done for him to want to humiliate me like that.

Life started to get more stressful. Not only did I have my panic and anxiety attacks that I had since I was a teenager, I also got acid reflux disease while with David. I didn't know what it was and thought I was having a heart attack one night. I finally went to the doctor. Nothing seemed to help curb the pain. When an attack came on, it felt like there was a huge knife in my chest clear through to my back and turning. It could last somewhere between ten to forty eight hours depending. This pain was in addition to the pain in my stomach that I felt from the time I was seventeen. I can describe it as two stones rubbing together right below my breast bone.

I did enjoy living in that apartment complex. It was pretty upscale, and there was a very large pool for which my daughter made full use of, and there were many interesting people.

There was a family from India. The mother walked at night, sometimes by herself, sometimes with her husband who was a professor at the University. They had two children. The woman fasted one day a week where she ate nothing, I assumed for twenty four hours, which I found interesting. I know we had many conversations and that our children played together, but don't remember much else. I know they moved to Pennsylvania for a short time before moving back to India. I still have letters from her saying how when they get back to India she wanted me to visit them and stay with them and would, "Get you many gifts." Years later I had tried to locate her but to no avail.

Another family was from Saudi Arabia. I don't know what the husband was studying. His wife was like a little girl, so quiet, so shy, and so innocent. She said we were sisters. They had a little boy who would come over to our apartment all the time. He really liked me as did his father. The father, not threatening at all but wanted me badly. He said many times he would divorce his wife. All he had to do was "Write it three times on something and give it to her family." He never touched me, nor made advances toward me. He was pretty obsessed with me but very respectful. I told him there was no way we could be together. I was married. I loved his wife and would never do that to her and he shouldn't even think of us together. They, too, were Muslim. One day some Seventh Day Adventists or Jehovah Witnesses came to their apartment while I was there, and I stupidly said, "They are Muslim!" and shut the door. Maybe they would have liked to hear about Jesus. I regret to this day doing that.

They, too, moved away. I barely remember when or how we said goodbye. I have a photo of when my daughter and I took them to a fireworks show one year. They seemed to enjoy that. After returning to their home country, they sent me a robe from Morocco and a gold ring with my name in Arabic engraved inside, and a gift for my daughter as well. I still have letters from him where he wanted me to come to Saudi Arabia or to Jidda where they vacationed. I did consider it, for a visit only; there was so much trouble in the Middle East though that I didn't want to risk it. I don't remember exactly which of these years my friends had left the U.S. but in 1981, Egypt's President, Anwar Sadat, was killed. An independent organization for the liberalization of Egypt claimed responsibility. They were against Sadat's policies including him signing a peace treaty with Israel in March, 1979. Pope John Paul II was shot by a Turk. The Lebanon War went on from 1982-1985 which involved the Israelis, Palestinians and the Lebanese. In '83 the U.S. bombarded Lebanon and then a few weeks later a U.S. marine barracks in Beirut was blown up by suicide truck bombs a couple of times. So, there was no way I was going to go to the Middle East with so much turmoil and unrest.

I have always said, "The first time I ever ate kiwi was on a bed with a bunch of Arabs!" I know that statement allows the imagination to go a bit wild, but it was with this family so not such a shocking event.

I also met some very good friends of theirs, also Saudis. The man was a large burly type. They had a little boy also and the wife. Oh my God, she was the most beautiful woman I have ever seen. Such a beauty. At first I wondered how she could be married to this big bear, but soon found out that he was so kind and generous and probably loved her dearly and treated her like a queen. They were always so happy. They moved to another town further south for him to finish his education. I was unemployed for a second time and I went to Lake Texoma with a friend to go boating and skiing. We stopped to visit this Saudi family, and when we were leaving the wife ran outside and put something in my hand. I didn't look until I was back in the car and we were driving away. They knew I was not working and she had slipped some money into my hand. To my surprise it was four one hundred dollar bills. I was truly surprised and grateful for the gift and thanked them many times over.

There were a few other foreign neighbors that I only greeted as I saw them. There was one couple whose shade of brown skin and their absolute beauty intrigued me. I couldn't figure out where they were from so I had to ask. They were from Ethiopia. Another apartment was occupied by some Arabs where the woman probably had actually worn the burqa all of her adult life. I remember going to visit them briefly about something, and the woman who opened the door I knew was the grandmother. She opened the door with her face exposed. Something in her eyes showed her age but not the skin of her face. Her garments had shielded her face from the sun and her skin was so smooth and silky it was hard for my eyes and mind to corroborate what I was seeing.

"You sure met a lot of interesting people. How was home life going?"

About 1981, David began building homes. He incorporated it, which was smart and I was the secretary treasurer for whatever that was worth. He asked me to help with naming the business. I came up with Celebrity Homes of course. He used it. I thought I would at least get a home out of the deal, but he never even took one for himself. A home was built and when all finished by the builders, I would go in to clean them. He would give me $50.00 a house. By all means and for the mess that the builders would leave and such a hard job, I probably should have been paid $1,000.00. I was still working at the copy place; this was more or less cheap labor for him and a little extra money for me.

"Were you still seeing Mario?"

Yes, but very, very little. I liked living with David because he didn't want the family around. It had become somewhat of a sanctuary. I would see Mario sometimes when David was at work at night, but my daughter and I were always home before he got there. I remember sitting sometimes in the parking lot in Mario's car at David's apartment. One time, when my daughter was about eight, I even sneaked out and had a late dinner with Mario and then to a hotel afterwards with him. I can't believe I left her home alone, but then she was one of those latchkey kids and was pretty much on her own to get to school and home every day. She was very smart also and never did anything stupid.

I remember that night very well. Mario had asked me previously if I would go out to dinner. He was entertaining some out of town friends that he wanted to impress was what I understood from the invite. I was pretty sick at the time with a cold or sinus infection. I tried to get out of the deal that day. He was so upset and mad. I finally agreed. It was an expensive restaurant that we had been to before, and for some reason I agreed to go to a hotel with him after knowing well that I wasn't up to having sex with him. He had had a few drinks of beer and was not taking no for an answer.

We did not have sex. Not only was I miserably sick, but he had a problem. "I have had women who could put a condom on with their mouth." I will never forget that. Well, I thought, "Good for you, but tonight because of your drinking, you can't even get it up." Of course I didn't say that. I know he had a lot of money and probably had in the past paid for some really great sex and experienced some fantastic pleasures but sorry, couldn't help him when he drank, it didn't work.

"So that affair went on for quite a while."

Yes, but that was about over. Mario had asked my mother once if David and I were really married. I don't think he believed me or wanted to believe it.

David must have known that I was seeing someone or some other men. He confronted me once and that is when I found out he was having me watched and followed. I didn't think it mattered what I was doing. The marriage was supposed to be on paper only. David was not making any commitments even though several months later we were still married. He made it quite clear what was and wasn't. Why was he having me watched? Maybe he didn't want to look like a fool.

So my affair came to an end with Mario and he didn't like it. He called the apartment one day and David answered. I was upstairs and I heard David cussing "Come over here you son of a bitch!" I had no clue who he was talking to at first. As the yelling and the cussing went on, I figured out that it was Mario. I became very frightened. David came upstairs and cussed me out or something, I don't really remember I was so afraid. I was afraid of David anyway, but this day I became terrified. To make matters worse, I went to the grocery store right after this and Mario must have actually been coming over to the apartment because he lived across town. When I pulled into the store parking lot, he pulled in behind me. He must have seen me leave the apartment and followed me. He approached me in the store parking lot and I was so terrified of David that I just tried to get away from him. I asked him to please go away. I guess I imagined David following me there and seeing us together. Mario couldn't understand. He was reaching for me and begging me to see him again. I told him I couldn't. That was the last time I ever saw Mario. It is sad; he was good looking, nice, romantic, and smart. I never wanted to hurt him but I did. I still have a couple of gifts that he brought back from Libya to me when he had traveled home a couple of times and some postcards that he sent on one of his travels around the U.S.

I almost got caught in the middle of one other incident while with David. He was studying architecture and building construction at the University. Well, one of his classmates that I did not know at the time was one of my Nigerian friends. And one day, David had mentioned that a classmate was going to come over to study with him and he told me his name. I nearly died. This friend of mine didn't know who I was married to, and I had seen him one last time also while I was with David. It was not that long after that he was coming to our house? I quickly came up with some excuse, probably involving my mother, so that I would not be there when he came over. I did manage to escape what could have been a most embarrassing and horrible altercation. I was thankful I had escaped that and grateful for getting off easy with the Mario affair.

"Did you like living on the edge?"

No, not at all. That's just how it seemed to be working out most of my life.

That was it though. I was done. No more screwing around. Whatever this was with David, it was there to stay for a while. With my fear of David, I realized I may have gotten into somewhat of the same situation as my mother did with Buss. I should have seen that coming for passing judgment on her.

I must have decided that David did love me in some way although he only said those words once. It was January 20, 1981. I remember because it was the day Ronald Reagan was sworn in to the presidency and gave his inaugural speech.

He didn't say it in the heat of passion or a sweet sentimental moment. We were having a discussion while still in bed that morning about us and our relationship. I think he said it something like this. "You want me to say I love you? I love you, there."

I know, I know, why did I stay with him? At first I did love him and I loved him for many years although we didn't always live together. Of the eleven and a half years that we were married, we lived eight of those in separate houses and only a few blocks away from each other. But then I was accustomed to living in a separate house.

I was sick most of the time while with David. The doctor said I had developed an ulcer on top of the acid reflux disease and anxiety attacks. I took medication for the ulcer for ten years. I was sick a lot, stressed beyond belief with him. He was a very unhappy man.

"He was unhappy?"

Oh yes, the most miserable, unhappy person I have ever come across. Nothing worked for him, nothing went his way, and people took advantage of him. I think he was always this way, but he says that he hated to leave his family. When he came to America, his father passed away but the family didn't tell him for quite a while. I don't think he ever got over that. He wanted to have at least gone back to Iran for the burial. I don't know why they kept it from him unless they were afraid for him to go back due to the discrimination toward the Jews. He told me they had to give up a couple of homes to the regime, so I assumed it was just a bad time for him to go back to Iran.

War broke out between Iran and Iraq in the 80's while we were married. The Iranians were sending boys as young as ten into the battlefields to detonate mines, David told me. He had a nephew about that age and the family and David feared for his life. Somehow with the help of David, he was brought to America and lived in New York City with family. David continued to help him financially, and David had even helped financially smuggle one of his brothers out of Iran and into Israel because his life was in danger for some reason. I sometimes think his heart was only big enough for his family and Iran, his homeland and he missed both very much.

CHAPTER SEVENTEEN

So our schedules were full. We both worked and had this business. I was pretty much completely unhappy also. We fought often. I just wanted him to be happy, make us all happy and love me. That was never going to happen. He didn't want a normal life. He didn't want to be married for real, and he never wanted children, although he acted like he wanted to be a part of my daughter's life. He made it clear that he wanted no children of his own. Unfortunately I got pregnant and he threatened to kick my stomach "until the baby would die".

"Oh my God!"

Now by this time I was in a situation probably not too unlike my mother's when she was with Buss. I was afraid of him, but loved him. He was mean and yet very likeable. He was a manipulator and we were his captives. He wanted to possess and control. I had tried to leave a few times, but he wouldn't let me. I wasn't sure if it was because he loved me somewhat or what the reason was because he surely didn't need me for anything. I thought he was better than all of this. I couldn't believe when he told me I better take care of it. In other words, get rid of it. I was so panic- stricken.

"Oh no, what did you do?"

Well, first since he wasn't going to let me leave, I started to work out the reasoning in my head as to why I had to have an abortion. I found out about the procedure and the cost. I tried to calculate as to whether it was David's or another's.

"I thought you had stayed faithful?"

I did except for one night that I spent at my sister's. David and I had had a fight. My daughter and I went there to spend the night, and her brother-in-law came over. I had been with him many years before and, well, I was very upset and distraught. He was comforting me and we ended up having sex. I still believe and believed then that it was David's by all calculations, but just in case, here was another reason. Had the child come out looking more like a Panamanian than an Iranian, he probably would have killed me.

I also figured I was stuck with him now but there may be a day that I can escape. But with a child, we all would be connected in some way forever. I thought he might even try to take the child from me. All I know is that there were so many more reasons to abort and to commit that mortal sin than to not. I needed to think of my daughter and myself and how to survive this mess I had gotten us into. Perhaps one day we would be out of the situation I got us into, but with his child I could not imagine ever being rid of him.

I didn't have the money so I asked a friend who I should have known would not lend me the money for such a thing. He was practically a preacher but I was desperate and didn't know of anyone else to ask, plus I didn't want anyone to know.

John was one of those goodie good guys that I had met years earlier when I worked at the convenience store. He would hang out almost every evening with me at the store just talking. Now he, I believe, could have loved me. We never slept together because I was not attracted to him, but then he never made a move either. He was a friend. We talked about so many things. He is the one that told me my stepfather was possessed when I described his eyes to him. He knew the bible and could quote verses. He was smitten with me. I rode with him once on his motorcycle and invited him to my house. We kissed and I let him touch my breast once, not bare, but he'd have to go to his grave with only that because that is all that had ever happened between us although I was very fond of him. He never married.

So John tried to talk me out of the abortion and also refused to lend me the money. I don't remember how I got the money together. I must have had it, but wanted to make sure I didn't come up short later on.

There were a lot of girls, women, in that office that day. I knew I was sinning terribly but God was just going to have to forgive me. I, too, was going to have to forgive myself one day. I went in, they put me out and I came to in the recovery room. I looked over at another girl and was shocked to see one of my high school friends just getting up from her recovery bed. She has since passed on. We talked about it once on the phone, but she said she didn't remember seeing me. I don't remember the month or the day. I know it was hot and I was in a lot of pain afterwards and tried to sleep away both the emotional and physical pain.

"I am so sorry but I know you were in a desperate situation."

It was done. David came home a few days later. I don't remember talking about it exactly. I do remember one time, long after the deed that I told David that I had gone to church when they had some bishops there to hear confessions. It might have been close to Easter. You know, we bad Catholics may not go to church all year, but by golly we go on Easter and Christmas.

I felt I had to confess this sin to a direct ear to God and this was the one opportunity I had. Several priests and bishops were seated openly around the altar. Parishioners lined up in the aisles and waited their turn. I bravely got in line with the rest. I didn't like the set up though. He was going to see me. I would have liked it better in the confessional booth but figured again, this is what you get. It's like facing God and you need to be held accountable for your horrid sin.

It was my turn. I can still see his face as I told him what I had done. He asked me about the father and I explained the situation and how he didn't want the child and threatened to kill both of us. With his kind compassionate eyes, under the circumstances, he pronounced me forgiven. I didn't feel forgiven and still don't. I still pray about it many times.

When I told David that I had gone to confession and confessed my sin he said something about how I had put it all on him now. I thought, "not my problem if you feel that way." "You need to go to God and get your own forgiveness," I said out loud.

The only other thing I ever remember David saying about it many years later was "It would have been a boy." He probably wished he had a son. He told me many times when and if we ever got a divorce, I had to become a nun. Sure. Had I become the nun when I wanted to, I would have never gone through such terrible things and become such a sinner.

I had a dream years later that seemed so real. It was of a young boy, probably about the age that this child would have been. This boy was dressed all in white satin-like clothes and very bright. The clothes reminded me of the painting of Little Boy Blue. He came over to my bed as I lay sleeping. There seemed to be a brighter shade of white around him as he slowly came closer to me. He was smiling. His face was pearly white and his hair brown and curly. I thought he was going to kiss me but I awoke.

"Did you tell anyone?"

I never told my family. I told my friends, Vinnie and Toine. They were on my payroll you know.

"Payroll?"

I say that jokingly. They never got paid for their love, concern, counseling and guidance throughout the years, but they were always there for me; especially Vinnie. I had known her since the ninth grade. She has never judged me and had known about almost everything I had been through since we met, always with an open ear and heart, and much needed advice. I may have not followed her advice, but she definitely helped me through many catastrophes. How fortunate for me that both were in the field of counseling. I don't know how I would have made it through my life without these two women and I thank God for their friendship.

I really went through a period of time after this that I really hated myself even more than before. I had a tendency to go into a deep depression once in a while and this brought on a good one.

"I know you got away from him, but how?"

Even though I wanted to leave so many times, he wouldn't let me. We had a fight one night and I don't even remember what we always fought about. This one night a friend of his was over and we were fighting, and he said "Get out!" and I left. I knew it was probably my one and only chance to get out. I knew he wouldn't do or say much more in front of his friend; frankly, I was surprised he was yelling at me while he was there. He must have really been mad about something, but I just don't remember what. I grabbed my daughter and we were out of there.

I must have gone to my sister's again because I know I didn't go to my mother's. I found an apartment I could afford and never moved back in with David. I did stay married to him though. We would go visit him and stay most weekends at his apartment. He had gone into the used car business and kept me in cars, but other than that, I wasn't getting anything from him. So even though I "got away," I wasn't really free of him. We lived in separate houses, but we still maintained some sort of relationship.

I got a good job at the University of Oklahoma after I moved out of David's. About a year or so later, I enrolled in a writing class at the University. This was my true passion after all, so I was very happy for the opportunity.

I met a young woman during this time. Her name was Susanne Lambdin who is a published novelist now. We were very close friends at the time. She could have been an adoptive aunt for my daughter; they liked each other that much. Susanne was so full of energy and youth. I was a bit jealous of her freedom and creativity, but loved her dearly and we laughed a lot. She was healthy for me. We had collaborated on a few creative ideas over a couple of years, but she went off to California soon after her graduation and worked at a couple of studios. She even wrote a script for a Star Trek episode. We lost contact at some time, but have since rekindled our friendship.

None of the family knew at the time but my brother, Don, had gone to a drug and alcohol treatment facility. I believe it was there that he found out he was HIV positive. It was 1985; he elected to tell me but no one else in the family, and he made me promise not to tell anyone, especially Mother. The only thing I knew about HIV was that it was pretty much a death sentence, and that I, so far, had been fortunate enough to not have contracted it.

I remained faithful to David and accomplished many things from then on. Over the years the weekend visits that started on Friday evening and ending on Sunday night had eventually gone down to Sundays only. I allowed my daughter to go over to his apartment more though; after all I felt he was her stepfather and I thought it was good for her to have a father figure, and I did trust him.

I was an extra sitting in a classroom in the movie "Offerings" that was shot in Oklahoma, and soon after that was hired to assistant direct a short film. I did more than assistant direct; I observed and thought there is nothing being done here that I couldn't do. Soon after that position and while still working at OU and raising my daughter and still dealing with Mother, her children and David, I started my own video production company. FIA/Films by Independent Artists, Inc. David revealed to me once that all of my "movie making stuff" took a lot of my time and he didn't like that, but what could he do especially when we didn't live together.

CHAPTER EIGHTEEN

I had a few screenplays written, and I wanted so much to produce them. I first started by advertising that I was looking for a crew. I knew that if I could do some short films or videos, I could try to get funding either through competitions or organizations. I lucked out right away with a man who worked at one of the local news stations. He had a camera that we could use. We had talked on the phone several times, and he invited me to a party the station was having. I asked a girlfriend, Shannon, to go with me. I had his name and when I approached the house I began asking for him. "Is Jim (so and so) here?" Some hadn't seen him yet. One guy asked me, "Oh, the black dude?" I said "No, I don't think so." But it was Jim, the black dude. I asked him how I couldn't tell on the phone that he was black, which didn't matter; I was just amused that I couldn't tell. He told me that his real ambition had always been to be a reporter and he had worked on not sounding black.

I got to meet some of the staff from the news station that night, and I had my camera guy and other equipment needed to start filming. I never asked if he was allowed to use this camera on the side, didn't want to know, figured he knew what he was doing. Considering the fact that we were allowed to use the news station's editing room all hours of the night when we were finished with this first short video, I again assumed he knew what he was doing.

Soon I had many young people who were more than willing to work on a film/video project. Then I advertised for actors and found plenty of them all willing and eager to work on a project even if there was no pay. They would get to do what they loved, and would be able to list it on their resume. They would also receive a copy of their work. That is all I could offer them, but they were more than willing.

Jerry Charles, a friend and accountant, became my production manager for my first short video in 1988. He was a true, much needed and appreciated friend. In his college days, he was an actor and performed in some plays. He said his best and longest role was playing a villain. This role, performed in Tulsa, lasted for years. From the look on his face, the twinkle in his eyes and such enthusiasm he has with the arts, you just know that acting was probably his greatest passion. His parents didn't think so, apparently, which sent him into several years of great depression. I think he kept trying to write off and on over the years also, but made his living as an insurance salesman and then a tax preparer/accountant.

An artistic person should never be discouraged or shut down from their talents. It is something that continually burns within that person and can be debilitating, depressing and cause anxiety. I don't think they are very happy unless they are pursuing their desires. At least that has been my observation.

Jerry married a woman named Rose, and he will tell you, "She is the love of my life." Anyone could surely tell these two truly loved each other. They had three children, and Rose died in 2010 from a freak accident. She was on a stretcher going to the hospital for something. A wheel on the stretcher broke and she toppled onto the cement. I believe she died from hitting her head on the cement.

Jerry had encouraged me many times even though he said, "You are a great writer, but you can't spell, CAT!" Can't criticize him for that, but after reading a book once about writers not being able to spell, I didn't feel too badly about myself.

I know that "Rachel" wouldn't have been produced without his help.

"Rachel?"

"Rachel" was the first screenplay I had written. We produced a trailer of this screenplay in order to try to get funding to do the whole movie. Rachel was about a faith healer in the late fifties. A young woman with eyes the color of honey named

Wendy took on the role of Rachel; she surely looked the part. She had a lengthy resume which included acting and singing. Wendy's singing talent was an added bonus for which my brain quickly found a way to use. Jerry and I found a congregation that was rehearsing for church services, and we asked if Wendy could sing with them and let us record them. They were a bit excited about the idea and let us take control of their rehearsing for about an hour or so.

Somehow many good things as well as stressful things happened while making this 17 minute trailer. Don't let 17 minutes of finished product fool you though. To come up with the finished product, we utilized about 8 shooting locations, rehearsals, several weekends of shooting, costumes, cars, and the coordination of about 15 actors and crew people, also extras when needed -- not to mention the hours and hours of editing. Jerry had gotten everything I needed from classic cars to a whole congregation for one of the brush arbor scenes.

"Guess I don't know what a brush arbor is."

I didn't either, but get this. My mother had purchased five acres in a really small town named Dibble south of Norman. I think she planned on moving out there one day but that never happened. In the meantime, over the years the family would go out there to just spend some time in the country. They also raised some watermelon and cantaloupe. Occasionally, I would go out there with them.

Well, there was this structure on the side of the road on the way to the acres. It was pretty much an open structure with some pews under it. Since I had written the screenplay, "Rachel," years before going out there, I would always say to myself whenever I shoot my film, "Rachel," I am going to use this spot for some of the scenes.

Jerry told me that a brush arbor was a structure that began in the seventeen hundreds with just enough coverage for a gathering of people to hold revivals and church meetings. So here was such a structure and as a result, thirteen years after I saw it, I did shoot some scenes there.

We had asked several people to come and be an extra for this one scene under the structure. I had hoped some would show. My daughter was with me, and I had picked up some of my friends' kids and we headed out to the location. They were dressed in fifties like clothes and I had my crew members, but that wouldn't be hardly enough. We had gotten permission from Dibble Baptist Church to use the brush arbor, and I had planned on catering lunch for anyone who showed up. I was excited to say the least.

My crew arrived. We located electricity, rearranged the pews and cleaned it up somewhat. One of my crew guys, Robert, climbed up into the roof area behind the stage. He hollered down to me. "Hey, there's a room back here!" I asked what was back there. "Well, some cots and an old piano." Bingo! That's exactly what I needed -- the piano. There was already a pulpit on stage. I was thrilled. Robert climbed down into the room and opened the locked door from the other side. We pulled the old, partly keyless piano out and we used the room as a dressing room. I couldn't ask for much more except those extras I needed to fill the pews. I was sure hoping and praying they would show.

We shot several scenes out in the field areas. I was getting frantic about no one showing up. Jerry finally said, "I'll bring back some extras." He and his son, Burt, left the area. About twenty minutes later here they came followed by several cars! I couldn't believe it! He had gone into this little town of Dibble and found a crowd of people at a soccer field. The game was about to end. I guess Jerry gave his best to convince them. These wonderful people came, signed a release form and sat through numerous takes and retakes. Some even acted as people going up to Rachel for extra blessings. It was great! We fed them a good lunch and thanked them graciously. A few days later I sent a note to their local newspaper thanking them for the use of the brush arbor and their local extras. I hope they know how much I appreciated everything.

By the way, we pushed the piano back into the room, locked it up and left the place a little neater. Hadn't been out there for years after that until my daughter moved out to my mom's acreage. Funny how for years it seemed like we had driven out there many times, a constant reminder to me of something I desired to accomplish, and once accomplished it didn't seem like a part of my life anymore.

"But it was."

Yes, I guess it was. It was a huge part of my life. Something that I had accomplished. A piece of a big dream and it left me wanting more.

"Nothing wrong with that."

Jerry introduced me to Toby Keith when we were finished with the trailer for "Rachel." Jerry had worked with Toby's father at one time in the insurance business and he knew Toby, his wife and children. Jerry really wanted me to produce the whole script of "Rachel" at that time. I was trying to get funding with the trailer and Jerry was thinking that we should get someone who is on their way to the top to be in the movie. Great idea, but I was going to have to do some rewriting in order to put Toby in the movie. I invited my friend Sherri to come over that night to meet Toby. She was a good friend at that time and also my financial advisor. I thought she would get a thrill out of meeting him. She did.

Toby is very tall. He seemed to be quiet and had a peaceful nature. He was kind and gracious with a really cute smile. He and his manager came to my house. We watched the trailer and talked. Toby was willing to be in the movie. His manager said they'd talk about it because Toby was getting ready to sign with Mercury Records and there may be somewhat of a problem. I watched Toby bend his head down to get out of my door as they left.

Copies of the seventeen-minute trailer of "Rachel" videos are in possession of friends, actors, crew members and myself. The script, still the same, is stored in my filing cabinet.

Not everything came easy or was easy when shooting this video. I was under a lot of stress. Still working full time, raising my daughter, and still dealing with Mother and David. I can't pinpoint or describe in detail what I was having to do for Mother; just that whatever they needed or any turmoil that would come up, I was there helping them.

David tried to divorce me somewhere in that time but didn't. He even called me one time from a lawyer's office cussing at me. I didn't argue with him and wished he had just gone ahead and gotten the divorce, but he didn't. I was drinking some then and calling Vinnie all hours of the night just to talk things through. God bless her.

Jim, my camera guy, was trying to screw the actresses and some of the actors and crew were getting close -- really close to each other, if you know what I mean. I started to understand how Hollywood people get involved with each other just from what I observed going on with my projects. Working so close and intensely for so many hours, people get close. The hours of preparation, rehearsing, shooting and the hours of editing, sometimes went on until about three in the morning. I had to be at work by eight.

Then there was this modeling agency, Fullerton, and some agent in Oklahoma City that was very interested in what I was doing. Jerry told me they were trying to get information of "this film being shot in Norman." I got the impression they didn't like it for some reason. I didn't know why but when "Rachel" was finished, Jim, my camera guy, got us a spot on a local morning talk show to tell what we were doing "in Norman." I didn't want to be interviewed so I asked a couple of my actors to do the interview and they were happy to oblige. When I found out they scrapped the idea, I put two and two together when I found out that the morning show host was friends with the owner of this modeling agency that was so concerned about my project. Jim did manage, however, to get a spot on the news about what we were doing. I had a wrap party and screening at a local restaurant and there were a couple of stories in the newspaper about the project.

Soon after the trailer of "Rachel," I heard that Fullerton was working on a film project and they hired Jim and most of my crew. Jim invited me on set one day. I walked in and a woman was sitting talking with some actors about acting. I don't remember what she said, but I for some gutsy reason, joined in on the conversation with a comment on how I would do whatever they were talking about. The young actors on the floor agreed with me.

This woman, who was with Fullerton, asked someone who I was. After a few hours of shooting, she asked to talk to me privately. She revealed that she knew who I was and was very interested in what I was doing; how I did what I did meaning "Rachel" and what were my future plans. I didn't give her much information when I felt she was just fishing, just wanting to get ideas, so I kindly told her, "If I ever need your services, say like if I ever need any actors for future projects, I might contact you to fax me some head shots" and I left. She made me feel like I needed to put her in her place so to speak, especially knowing that they didn't like what I was working on. They managed to scrap the morning show interview and hired my people.

Jim told me she was kind of upset after I left and closed the set, meaning that no one was to be around that wasn't connected with the making of their film. He said when she found out I had written the screenplay and was also directing my work, she fired their director and she became the director and tried to change some of their script. I never did ask her for any headshots for my other works. I was provided with a copy of their project and heard it was in the can. I never heard any more about Fullerton doing such projects.

Time moved on. My daughter was in her senior year and dating a Persian boy that David had introduced her to. I continued to work at the University and tried to apply for funding to produce all of "Rachel." I helped my friend Lisa write a play for her class requirement before graduating, and also co-wrote a screenplay with a college professor for Lisa, based on a character that she wanted to portray. He got paid; I wanted royalties should it ever have gone into production.

My brother Don grew thinner and on a couple of occasions he would come to Norman to visit Mother. He was on a regiment of drinking what they called a cocktail every two hours during the night. He, not wanting Mother to know he had AIDS, asked if I would also spend the night there so that I could wake him to take his medicine. I have trained myself to wake up at any given time, day or night, and I trusted it completely. I never failed and she never knew.

I even started to take Mother to Tulsa to visit Don, but had to call ahead to make sure he was not showing any other signs of the disease. I often wanted him to tell her but he just didn't want to. His roommate called me one day and told me Don was in the hospital. My daughter and I were actually going to go out of town to a nature park, but I changed my plans and drove to Tulsa to see how he was doing.

Another time he was in the hospital, I found him encircled by parishioners from a non-denominational church he had been attending. I joined hands and prayed with them. Even though I had gone to Tulsa to see him occasionally since his illness, this was the first time that I knew it was bad. With his fellow worshipers gone, I began to talk to Don. He seemed as though he had energy and was in good spirits, but his mind was not clear. I said, "Don, I think it's time to tell your mother." I always referred to her as "your mother" to my siblings as in kind of a joke. Without hesitation and a huge smile on his face he said, "You think so? Okay." It was as if a huge weight had been lifted from his shoulders, and I knew he expected me to be the one to tell her.

Now from the beginning I told both Don and his roommate, "I am not going to be the one to tell her," and I repeated it and stressed over it for five years.

David had let me take a truck from his car lot this time to see Don. When I started to drive home that weekend after apparently setting my brother's mind at ease, and just after getting onto the turnpike, the truck started to sputter as if out of gas. I pulled over to the side of the highway. It was extremely windy that day, but I never thought I would find flames coming out from around the steering rod. The wind was whipping under the fender. I slammed the hood down and started to hurry away from the truck. I thought about my wallet and other things in the truck, so I hurried back and grabbed what I could. Now in my mind I didn't know how much time I had because I only had to judge by what I had seen on TV. So, not much time before the flame would get to the fuel tank and explode.

The truck hood and fender walls were swirling in smoke as I hurried away again from the truck, then I thought of all the drivers that were going to make that curve and possibly get hurt when the truck explodes, so I again made my way closer to the truck and started to wave to warn other drivers. Soon a Good Samaritan pulled over and I hopped into the vehicle. We drove to a poll booth and told them that my truck was on fire. When this person took me back to the truck, it was fully engulfed in flames and fire trucks were already there trying to put it out.

It was obvious there was nothing I could do, so these good people asked if there was somewhere they could take me. I asked them to drop me off at a McDonald's just off the turnpike. I called my brother's roommate to pick me up. I was dreading calling David. When I did, he bitched and cussed like a crazy man. He didn't carry insurance on his vehicles on the lot. He was infuriated that he lost money, and he was going to have to come and get me the next day. I told him I would catch a bus to Oklahoma City and he could pick me up there. That way instead of hearing him bitch at me for two or three hours, it would only be about thirty minutes as we drove back to Norman. I think he blamed me more for going to Tulsa than for burning his truck up. Basically he knew about Don and he knew it wasn't my fault, but he had to take his anger out on someone.

The next day I gathered up my sister because she was a home health nurse, and by this time she knew of Don's disease but honored his wishes in keeping it from Mother also. I thought Mother would surely have a heart attack and I wouldn't know what to do to help her. I couldn't believe I was going to have to tell her that her son was dying. Her favorite child only had a few months to live. I remember telling her that Teresa had some weird stomach thing once and she was very upset, always with the drama. Then she turned right to my face and yelled she wished it was me and not Teresa -- her second favorite child.

We arrived at her house and sat her down and I began to say, "Don is in the hospital and..." she finished my sentence, "He has AIDS doesn't he?" I was taken aback and I thanked the Holy

Spirit for giving her this wisdom and allowing it to come from her mouth and not mine.

She decided she would go to Tulsa and stay with him. We siblings also would go to visit for the next three months off and on. His moods were mostly good when we visited, and he talked of silly things in the past as if they were in the present. He talked of being out in the garden and picking vegetables or about giving away a car that day at the radio station. One time he thought there was an Indian in his room and then realized, "That was silly, wasn't it?" I thought how merciful is God to let him experience happiness instead of the thought of dying. I personally didn't know that AIDS could affect the brain, but was grateful that except for his thinness he had no other signs of the disease.

I got the call from hospice to rush to Tulsa. Mark and Fred had been to visit Don a few days prior so they decided not to go this time. I don't think they wanted to be there for the end. My sister and daughter rode to Tulsa with me. We had only a short time with him before he went into that coma like state. Teresa and I decided we would estimate where his spirit would be looking down at himself when he passed and decided to wave at him. Kind of silly but we three were kind of silly that way and he would have liked it. We took turns sitting with him. Mother decided to rest sometime in the middle of the night. I sat beside him and began talking to the hospice nurse about him. I talked about what a good brother he was and some silly things. Then I started to tell her about his career, the only one he ever had, being a Deejay and how much he loved it. She and I noticed a half smile on his face. She said, "He can hear you." That should have been my cue to talk to him directly and tell him how much I loved him or something but I couldn't do it. The thought of it made me feel embarrassed.

"Afraid you'd be judged?"

Yeah, I guess so. I was quiet for a few moments. The nurse got out of her chair and came over to us. She moved his position and he started to begin breathing deeper and quicker. It was time. I hurried to get Mother and Teresa, and I asked my daughter if she wanted to be there. She declined. We gathered around Don's bed as did his roommate.

I had never watched a person die. I thought it seemed a bit painful for him. Mother was in the chair beside him. I was trembling as I bent down to hold her as he took his last breath and exhaled long and steady. Teresa and I remembered to turn and look up to the ceiling as silly as we felt and waved. Mother sat there for a while. When the ambulance arrived I took Mother into the other bedroom so she wouldn't have to see him being moved onto the stretcher. I observed her as she just sat on the edge of the bed looking downward. I was waiting for the drama but there was none. She just sat there in her own thoughts and feelings.

Don's friends arranged for the ceremony at the non-denominational church. There were quite a few friends from high school as well as business associates over the years. David attended as well. In order for us to be able to take Don home with us that day, we needed to pay for the cremation and urn that I had picked out. David wrote a check and I got a loan when I got back to Norman to pay him back.

"Your mother didn't pay for anything?"

No. She didn't have the money and besides she always let me take care of everything. With me around she never had to worry about anything she knew I would take care of everything.

"I wonder if you took on that role or did she manipulate you into the responsible one because she didn't or couldn't be a responsible person."

If I took it on, I must have at a very early age possibly realizing that she wasn't going to be the mother. If she manipulated me into that position at an early age, what kind of person does that?

I had to make another trip back to Tulsa soon after Don's passing to collect his personal belongings as well as his car. Mother came to my home after I had gotten back so she could take his things including the car to her house. She was sitting in my living room chair and I had just gotten back. I don't remember what was said, but she began to pull one of her dramatic scenes. She started to cry loudly and slip from the chair onto the floor. I yelled at her that I wasn't going to put up with her drama, that things happen, etc. I don't know exactly what I said but I was loud and stern. She immediately changed her composure, straightened up and left my house.

Many times later she blamed me for not telling her about Don having AIDS -- that she only had those last few months with him. She thought he was sick because he was losing weight but never thought it was that. She hated me for not telling her. She never understood that he didn't want her to know for whatever reason and it was not my place to tell her.

So therefore I wrote a short script, "Unspoken," and took a directing course at OU. This script was written for a few reasons. One for me to be able to get out what I was holding inside about my brother Don's death, and for my mother to know how I felt about how she didn't know or was in denial of his sickness. I also wanted to use it to try to get funding to produce the whole screenplay, "Rachel."

Script was written and I began again in the same manner to look for actors and crew. I was going to use Jim again for my camera guy when he was finished with Fullerton, but he became more arrogant. There were other girls on this project that I didn't want to be hassled by him if he were to continue to act as he did on the other project. Jim also wanted to put his name on the credits as a producer, which he wouldn't be. So I let him go. I had faith in God that another camera guy would come along and miraculously another did. My friend Cindy just happened to know this brilliant young man who could shoot, edit and create great things with a computer. Michael was eager and agreed even though there was no money. He didn't have camera equipment, but told me where I could purchase some at wholesale prices. I purchased a high dollar Hi 8 camera almost as big as the ones used by the news stations. I got lights, cords and microphones and was ready to go. I was in debt, but happy I was being creative.

I didn't divulge at first to my crew that this script pertained to my brothers passing and things that weren't said but when I did, they became closer to the project. They said they were glad I told them that they would be acting out not only him, but me as well, and it meant more to them. Many of them knew him from the radio. One night I had everyone over to go through the many tapes of Don that he had recorded while Deejaying. I was looking for clips that I could use at the end of the video.

Most of "Unspoken" went without a hitch. Most was shot at my friend Cindy's house. A local funeral home let us use one of their people and a hearse, and two of my girl actors had posed in a college playboy issue that year. Lavon portrayed me in the video; she had cut her hand pretty badly the night before our shoot. She had been in the ER all night, but still showed up at 4:30 a.m. to begin shooting. Her mother, Teri who was a good friend of mine, portrayed my mother and did an awesome job.

Michael and I had joined the college cable network as producers to edit some of our work and to broadcast it on air which we had accomplished. Soon after we were kicked out when they found out that Michael had plugged some cables in different hookups as he thought they should have been.

I had a man in LA that was working at being my agent for whatever that was worth. He informed me that after sending "Unspoken" to him, there were parts that were being used in some promo out there for or about AIDS. I took his word for it.

Not too long after this, David, his friend that was dating my daughter, myself and daughter were sitting in the living room of my house just visiting. My daughter's boyfriend made a response directly to me about something that was said by David. It had something to do with my daughter not getting hurt. I didn't understand what he was trying to tell me that night but found out soon after.

My daughter, just a few months from turning eighteen came into my bedroom one night and sat on the edge of the bed as I was doing something by my dresser. "I have to tell you something about David and me." Without hesitation I asked, "What, are you sleeping with him?" "No, No!" She was shocked at my question. But she did inform me something to the fact that at some time when she was a few years younger, he had started to touch her inappropriately.

    I didn't get the details. She had told her boyfriend and he convinced her to tell me. I took a valium that had been prescribed for me a few years previously. I hardly ever took one, but knew I had to take something as the rage in me rose. I drove over to David's apartment, went in and confronted him loudly and abruptly, and then turned to leave. He tried to grab me to keep me in the apartment. I got away twice as I made my way to the door and out into the parking lot still yelling at him. He didn't want a scene and cowered back into his apartment. I took another pill and not sure if I drove over to my friend Sherrie's that night to tell her about it or if that was another night.

"Understandable."

    I demanded a divorce and some money from David, and got both without a hassle. It was 1990. We had been married eleven and a half years. He didn't really deny anything much but wanted to talk to my daughter but she refused. He wrote her a letter and he wrote me several proclaiming how he loved us and we were his family and how without me he was all alone.

    I could not believe that he had done anything; I would never had expected that from him. Any other man but David. I tried to be so careful and failed again, failed my daughter.

    It's not something my daughter and I have ever really talked about. I asked her if she wanted to press any kind of charges. I would have done whatever she wanted. She didn't. I let my friend Vinnie talk to her. I remember one afternoon when the two of them were talking, I must have asked Vinnie a question. She said she couldn't tell me -- that whatever my daughter was telling her was confidential. I was so angry and upset about the whole thing, I sternly said, "Damn you!" to my very best friend ever. I, of course, apologized sometime later. I know she knew I didn't really mean it. I just couldn't believe the thing I watched for so carefully kept happening to my poor daughter in some form. I do know that Vinnie told her that I looked and watched so hard that I just didn't see. I also found it hard to understand why my daughter didn't tell me whatever was going on until I realized that he knew just how to control and manipulate her and had been doing that since she was just about five years old. And I'm sure he threatened her or me over the years and she was afraid.

I went to talk to a psychiatrist. I didn't tell her all the details but she thought I should be on some kind of meds. I left and never went back. I was having a terrible time trying to deal with what had happened. I felt that if I could think of my daughter as a friend and not as my daughter, I might just be able to accept what had happened to her and get through the worst of the pain.

As hard as that was to deal with and go through, we both made it. My daughter graduated high school and I was coping the best I could under the circumstances. A few months previous though, there had been some changes at work. A woman who was the office manager had decided to make some strange demands on us. One was that we ask to go to the restroom. Now I am not the kind of person that just conforms to what I consider ignorant rules, and I am not the kind of person that will cooperate with such stupidity. It was not the kind of office that warranted such a requirement under any circumstance. She also began to ask each one of us into her office to basically rat on each other.

When my turn came one day, I refused to say anything about anyone and told her, "Look, I come here to do my job the best I can and go home. I don't have anything to say about anyone and I am not going to ask to go to the bathroom. I will let you know when I am going, but will not ask permission."

She didn't like that. In fact she hated it so much that she began to make a case against me. A few weeks went by and one day I was called into the boss's office. She had come up with thirteen pages of complaints against me. Of course, it was like an outline and then details about each thing -- from me being rude to customers, getting printing orders wrong, always on the phone and never there. It would have been comical if it was a year or so later, but not at this time. In fact I was so devastated that I actually went home, drove into my garage, shut the door and sat in the car as it continued to run.

I was tired, simply tired of everything and I couldn't think of anything to keep me here. Nothing, not my daughter who I loved more than anything, not even the belief that I would go to hell if I committed suicide. I have no idea why I finally turned the key off.

I sucked it up like everything else and went back to work. This office manager suggested, not made it mandatory, I take some kind of courtesy phone etiquette class offered by the University for which I had already taken some time previously, so I didn't. Six months later they decided to either terminate me or have me resign. She said I hadn't improved, was never there and didn't take that phone class.

I asked if I could make a phone call before I made that decision. She and my boss wanted me to make it in front of them, but I told them I would make it in another office. I called my friend Jerry, the accountant, and asked if I would get unemployment if I resigned. I didn't want to get fired, I wanted to resign. He said probably not unless I fought for it and it could take about six months.

I thanked him, walked into the other room where they were waiting for me and I told them I would resign. I signed the paper and left. I walked over to the personnel office and talked with a woman who was fond of me (as most people) and told her what had just happened. She was very sorry, didn't understand and said, "I worked for the employment office for eleven years and there is no way you will receive unemployment." Then she said, "Wait here a moment." She was gone for a few minutes and when she came back she said, "I can't believe it, they are going to allow you to receive unemployment." By "they" I assumed whoever "they" were, they weren't going to deny my request when I filed.

At this point I knew they were wrong and I had the upper hand. I filed for unemployment and I also talked with the affirmative action office at the University. They said I had ten days to file a complaint. I considered it for days. I was also getting calls from one of the women I worked with. I knew she only called to find out if I was going to file a complaint against the department.

I really wasn't sure for a few days, but made this person

believe I was going to up until the ten days had past. I had really considered it, but I thought I would eventually be blackballed from the University and I was not going to let that happen. I had too many people that could give me a good reference and I would get another job at the University. I had no doubt about that.

I took some time off, collected my nine months of unemployment and then went back to OU and took a job within the temp agency until I found a job that I really wanted within the University.

I continued to be creative and run my business. Many jobs came after "Unspoken" and with Michael by my side. He was very creative, energetic, willing to do anything for practically nothing and be my friend. He was also a magician and kept me and my friends entertained.

We shot dance recitals, promotional videos for charitable establishments and sample commercials for individuals. Lisa, who I had known since she was a child, wanted to be involved in whatever I was doing, so I let her be the spokesperson in a charitable promo for a horse riding ranch for children with disabilities. I also shot some mock commercials so she could promote herself in addition to helping her write an adaptation of "The Velveteen Rabbit" for one of her college courses and co-writing that screenplay. Lisa had even gotten a stage actress and acting coach from LA to come to Oklahoma. We held a weekend class where I shot their scenes for them and gave them the tape. These projects I did for no fee because she was a friend, and also we had discussed opening our own school for acting.

At some point Lisa started to work for that Fullerton Modeling Agency. Around 1992 or 1993 they had assigned her to take pictures of activities going on during the filming of "Rise and Walk; The Dennis Byrd Story," in Norman. Some of the movie was shot at the University of Oklahoma's football stadium and lockers. There were also scenes filmed at the local hospital.

Lisa had met Dennis Byrd and Dan Lauria. Dennis was from Oklahoma City, played professional football for the Jets in 1990 but suffered a shattering neck injury. They said he would be paralyzed and never walk again, but with vigorous physical therapy he was able to.

Dan is probably most known for his role as the father on "The Wonder Years." Apparently Dan and Lisa had talked about theatre and acting and Lisa had mentioned me and my writing and video business. She had arranged for us to meet one evening. Lisa and I went to the stadium and waited for the locker room scene to end. If you've ever been to a shooting, you know it takes forever sometimes. It was cold and windy as Lisa and I waited just outside the locker room. We could hear their lines as they shot the same scene over and over again. We chatted with a few of the other actors and crew as they waited around for the end of a long day. We were invited to eat their food that was assembled on long tables, but since we were going to take Dan to dinner we refused.

Finally, Dan walked out to greet us. Now, long before this night, I had become quite fond of his character in, "The Wonder Years," so when he walked out, I immediately felt very comfortable and close to him. "I just need to change before we take off, if you can meet me at the trailer," he said.

As Lisa and I drove around to the trailer, it started to rain. I hate driving in the rain, especially at night, and with Dan, I thought I'd be a nervous wreck. Dan jogged out to the car, sat in the front with me. We first talked about going somewhere in Norman to have dinner and talk about this idea Dan had about a Regional Theatre that Lisa and I could start. I wanted to stay in Norman, but Dan wanted to go back to Oklahoma City to the Marriott where he was staying. I didn't have enough gas to get to the city so I pulled over at a convenience store and as I reached for my wallet, Dan jumped out of the car, "I got it!"

It was pouring by now and the wind was blowing harder; it was quite miserable. We were under an awning but I knew he was still getting wet. I couldn't believe Dan Lauria was not only in my car, but paying for and pumping gas in my car. I thought what a nice, down to earth guy.

On our drive to OK City, which took about forty-five minutes or so in the pouring rain, we listened to some jazz and blues tapes I had in the car. We talked about music and how he, too, liked the blues and we talked a little about the theatre idea. He and I said something about being Italian and feeling the music. I am sure Lisa was feeling a bit left out, especially when Dan and I laughed about something and I, just by a natural, friendly reaction, touched his leg. I felt as if I had known him for years. I wasn't nervous about the drive or anything for that matter.

We arrived at the Marriott, but didn't get anything to eat. Instead we went into the club, Russells, and we all ordered a beer. It was a weeknight so the place was not very busy. Music played and occasionally a couple or two would get up to dance. I poured a little beer from my bottle into a glass as I always do. My habit is to sip from the glass until it is empty, and then when ready, pour another small amount into the glass. Dan said, "That's the way my father drinks his beer! I've never seen anyone else do that." "Really? If I drink beer, I use a glass, and by pouring a little, well it just seems more ladylike and it stays colder, longer." "Yeah," Dan said. "That's why he does it, the cold part." We laughed.

I looked at the scars on his handsome face as he talked a little about being a marine. I thought how he seemed much like his character on the show. He talked fondly about Christian Slater and I sensed a father son kind of relationship between them. We also talked at length about setting up a Regional Theatre. He said he and Alley Mills, the woman who played his wife in "The Wonder Years," would perform opening night for our first play to get the theatre started. The theatre would be to bring in name actors and give local supportive actors a great opportunity.

I thought it was a great idea and was really gung ho. Lisa, on the other hand, worried too much and was afraid. I say if you want to do something bad enough, try it, go for it. If it doesn't work, well at least you tried. I did some research into the matter, waited for her to get on board, but it never came about. I could have done a lot of the behind the scenes work, but I needed her for the PR work. It would have been a lot of work for me. Even though I was stretched in several directions, I would have gone for it for sure. Maybe we could have done it, maybe not.

"That's too bad. It sounds like it would have been a great accomplishment."

I continued to work at the University of Oklahoma through the temp department and started to date. I had met a couple of young men. Nothing serious and I did not sleep with them. I was dating men that were about ten years younger than I, and my daughter was dating men that were six or seven years older than her. One day she jokingly said something about being concerned that I might like some of her boyfriends. "That would never happen," I told her, "because we have different tastes in men. I like them cute." My daughter liked men with strong features, like big chins, or large noses.

"Do you think you were seeing younger men to be in control or not wanting to get serious?"

Probably both. I was enjoying my freedom from David that's for sure. That was eleven and a half years of my life. Eleven and a half years of more hell on top of hell. My daughter was grateful for the end of that life also. I just wish she had told me a lot sooner and I would have gotten us out of that situation immediately upon knowing of the liberties he took with her.

I landed a good job with the Energy Department at the University and soon after, started seeing a man named Brent. He was about the same age as I, Catholic and had a good job at General Motors. He was very sweet, kind, attentive and fun. Our relationship seemed to be somewhat serious, and after a few months he took me to New Orleans for a week. I can honestly say that trip was probably the first time I had ever had real fun and relaxation in all of my adult years up to that point.

Brent had been staying with me three to four days out of the week for a couple of months. We had great times and had even started to write a screenplay together. One day I came home and he wasn't there; and, I noticed that his bag of personal items were gone. I was talking to a friend on the phone and saw a key on the living room floor. Ah, so he had left, tossed the key onto the floor, locked the door from the inside and was gone.

"How long did that relationship last?"

Nine months. I would have never expected him to just

leave like that -- no explanation. We did talk on the phone about him just leaving like that. He was being transferred he said. I called his mother in Michigan and she revealed truths to his lies, so eventually I was all right with his departure.

"Such as?"

Well, he was not a Green Beret who served in Vietnam, and as a child he was in special education classes, and his seizures were not a result of Agent Orange. Regardless, his departure kind of broke my heart. I had never, ever been dumped, and it didn't feel good at all.

I swore off men, went to work and came home, and never went out for about fifteen months. My girlfriends tried to get me out of the house, but I refused.

During this time I got another job with the University -- a joint project between the University and Department of Human Services -- a new training and development program for DHS employees. They called it SATTRN. I was working as a temp and was hired under contract. My position was a site coordinator. I came highly recommended by my previous employers at the Energy Department.

It was a good forty five minute drive give or take to Oklahoma City. At first I really hated the hectic drive, but they allowed me to come in and leave work a little later so I could avoid most of the traffic both ways. I really enjoyed the sunsets as I made my way home. Some nights I would compare them to sunsets in Africa, as seen on tv of course.

On my first day they gave me a pen, a date book, a desk and phone, and they explained what they were trying to accomplish for this new endeavor. Basically, the program was a continued method of training DHS employees throughout the state. That meant for me setting up good communication and smooth operations of scheduling training sessions, enrollment, setting up and troubleshooting their new satellite systems, distribution of VHS tapes, and continued meetings and brainstorming.

"For the whole state?"

Yes. That is seventy-seven counties; I figured it up once. I had to email and or call, talk to and help with any problems that came about pretty regularly with around two hundred thirty (230) people, mostly supervisors and directors.

Alice was a county director. I had helped her several times over the phone and emails. I had met her once when she came to Oklahoma City to be in one of the training videos that we were shooting at our office. I was very busy that morning with a group of people coming in to watch a program, but I managed to pop in before they started shooting. I said hi to her and introduced myself. I didn't realize the elderly woman I greeted in the front office was possibly her grandmother until after they had left. I didn't even know that Alice was Reba McEntire's sister until later on – one day someone had mentioned it. Then I recognized the resemblance and the strong Okie accent.

I had thought a few years before about getting a script to Reba, if I should ever write one with her in mind. But how would I get it to her. Well, my friend Cheri had a very good friend who is Reba's neighbor in Nashville. Cheri had told me that if ever that would come up, she would ask them to get a copy to Reba. Well now, here was Reba's sister, wow!

"But no script."

Yeah, no script. Sometime later after leaving that job, I was hired by the University to videotape a leadership course. This was through my own business, Film's by Independent Artist's, Inc.

I was waiting in the hotel lobby for my cue to go in and set up. A woman came walking by and said, "That speaker is about to wear me out." I said, "Me too, and I'm only hearing parts of it." She went into the restroom and returned back into the seminar room. I thought, "I've seen that woman before." I couldn't place her until I went into the room to set my camera and other equipment up. Then I realized it was Alice. I reminded her who I was. She said, "Oh yeah, nice to see you again." That was it. She was one of the keynote speakers. When that part of the course was over, she was out of there in a split second.

The next morning out at what is called the Ropes Course Field, I was setting up my camera. Alice walked over and started talking to me. We discussed the SATTRN project. We talked about some of its pros and cons, and then she asked me what I would charge to shoot a music video for a singer out of Utah. She said she had sent a singer to Narvel, Reba's husband, and he was already on his way to Nashville. She told me to watch for him, but I don't remember the name. In my mind I was thinking, "She must filter through people occasionally for Reba and Narvel and send good talent their way." I said, "Alice, I would shoot that video for you for nothing if you would get a script to Reba, if I should ever write one for her. I know she likes goody-good ones and I've thought about it for years, but haven't come up with anything yet." She replied, "Yeah, but you need to make some money on the deal also." I told her we'd talk about it. I offered to take her to dinner the next evening. Sad to say, we couldn't arrange dinner that evening, but on the last day of their leadership training, I was invited to eat with them. I sat with Alice and a few other DHS directors that I knew. We didn't get to talk much about the music video, but talked about our daughters and other such things. I gave Alice my business card and she said she would contact me whenever she got things arranged.

Over several months and even a few years, we were always going to have lunch. She never needed me to shoot the music video. She gave me her daughter's phone number so I could send her a sample of my CD of lyrics with music set to them from a company in Nashville.

"Oh, I didn't know about your music."

Yeah, well nothing came from that either. This company was also supposed to try to promote your music but doubt that they really spend much time doing that. Alice's daughter was very gracious, and even though she had gotten out of that scene, said she would see what she could do.

Years later and after no contact with Alice, I finally called her. We met for lunch and have continued to stay in touch.

CHAPTER NINETEEN

Just about fifteen months after Brent left me, I was in a bar, early, waiting on a woman named Terrie who looked a bit like Reba McEntire. She said she could sing like her also and she wanted a music video to send off to a competition of some sort. I noticed a guy playing pool by himself and one other person in the bar besides the bartenders. I sat waiting for Michael and this woman and her boyfriend to arrive. After about fifteen minutes the guy playing pool came over to me, asked if he could buy me a beer and if I would like to shoot some pool with him. I thanked him, but from what I saw, I thought, "Who the hell does he think he is talking to me?"

"Still done with men?"

Well yes, that, and he looked like a nerd in western attire, but he seemed nice. After waiting another ten minutes or so, I did go over to the pool table and accepted a beer. He introduced himself and asked what I was doing and I told him why I was there. Finally everyone arrived. We shot take after take after take of Terrie and her boyfriend dancing to one of Reba's songs and this guy, I'll call M.C. stood close by watching.

A couple of my girlfriends came out to the club to see how the work was going. As we finished they told me to stay and party with them. I really didn't want to, but since I was there I decided to stay and try to have some kind of fun. The whole night M.C. stood by and wanted to dance with me and talk with me. I didn't know how to two step so I declined. I really was just having a good time talking with my friends and having a few drinks, especially since it was the first time I had been anywhere since Brent had left.

Turns out this country western club was kind of a fun

place, so my friends and I began to frequent it often. M.C. was there another time or two, and we did dance and talk. I was kind of getting used to him. He seemed very nice and likeable.

I ended up getting another job at the College of Business at the University. I remember the first day. I arrived on time and had to wait on the person who would be my boss. When she walked in, I saw this much younger than me cute blonde. At first it was hard for me to accept a younger person being over me, but liked her almost immediately. Carrie was very sweet and I think she thought I was weird but interesting. She would have these lists of things for me to do for which I did, but I often wondered what she was doing in her office. One day, and she will amusingly tell you, that I was standing in the doorway to her office and asked her, "Are you going to do anything today?" But then again she can confirm the story that one day I went into her office, sat down and said, "I thought I had all the friends I ever needed or wanted but I found that I wanted one more." We have been friends ever since.

It was while working for this department that I was able to meet Michael Dell of Dell Computers, Ted Turner and Jane Fonda. The College of Business held a large conference in an Oklahoma City hotel and they were attendees. Mr. Dell and Mr. Turner were keynote speakers. I, of course, was more interested in meeting Jane.

I had some running around to do before the conference meetings started and was a bit frazzled. I was able to get into the hallway where many people were standing looking into a large greeting room. I noticed two guards standing by a door to a room. I assumed it was Jane's room. She came out wearing sunglasses and I noticed she walked with her head down, the guards by her side and a bit in the lead. She had a destination in mind and knew how to get there without being hassled. I assumed this was common practice. I watched as she entered the crowded greeting room, found a spot quickly, turned around, smiled big and greeted everyone with a cheerful hello. I stood in the hallway trying to see over and through some of the people until I thought, I am going in. I boldly made my way through the crowd and into the greeting room. I noticed Ted at the bar talking to many people, but set my sights on Jane. I walked over to her, introduced myself and my position, as if she knew me. I must have still looked frazzled because as she rubbed my arm she cheerfully said, "Oh, it'll all be over soon." I laughed, thanked her and moved on to briefly meet Ted.

I don't want to detail M.C.'s and my relationship, but there was one. I knew two years into the relationship when I caught him cheating several times, that it wasn't going to work, so I left him in the spring of '96.

I had moved to another town with him, so therefore when I wanted to move back to Norman, I had nowhere to stay. Believe it or not, I went home to Mommy.

"Hard to believe. How did that go?"

Oh my God, it was terrible. All she and Eldon did was fight. She would drink and he would smoke his pot and she would nag him to death. Just as with Buss -- she would never shut her mouth.

I was pretty desperate in wanting to know what I should or what I was going to be doing in the near future. M.C. and I were still at least talking on the phone, but I didn't know what to do about us. I called on an earthly being that just possibly could tell me something that I needed to know. Now was the important thing. I needed to have some word on the now. I had prayed and pleaded with God as before to please give me some answers, but you know how long that can take, and I was really too tired and desperate to cope any longer.

The woman, Joni, was an actress who had played a preacher in my video, "Rachel." My friend, Meredith, had told me that Joni could read Tarot Cards and tea leaves. I knew it was wrong, but went anyway. Meredith was also in "Rachel," and she also owned a beauty salon for which she and her staff contributed their talents for hair and makeup for my 50's trailer. She, too, became a very good friend of mine. Meredith is one of the most generous women I have ever known.

I arrived. Joni was ready to get started right away. I sat

across from her at the kitchen counter. After greeting her dogs and small chit chat, we were ready to proceed. She told me to shuffle the cards just so and think of a question about what I wanted. I really don't care for those cards. I didn't tell her this at first. I think they are really satanic and perhaps that is why they weren't working for me after two tries.

She took my right hand and began to look at its lines. Now this I might believe. As she inspected my lines, these are the things she came up with: I was very talented and abused as a child. I was here to deliver a message, as she pointed out the distinctive M in the middle of my hand. My talent, my inner self and my past were all trying to join together. I immediately thought, "Yes, my book." Through these three things, I will deliver my message or messages.

She asked if my mother was still alive and I said yes. She frowned. She said simply, "Enjoy her." I asked, "What?" She said enjoy the time you'll have with her because she didn't think that she would be here much longer.

Joni went on to tell me that I needed to help my mother set her mind at ease. To help her write out a living will and get other things in order. "She worries about these things. She worries that she would be a burden to her children if something should happen to her." I didn't think this was accurate due to mother's actions. My mother had recently told me that the doctors had found a very small tumor close to her brain. Her heart was bad. She had no energy and had been passing out. I had previously talked to my friend Vinnie about these passing out episodes. She said it sounded as if mother was having mini strokes and that she could continue to have them or she could have one massive one.

I didn't know if any of that was true. I sometimes wondered what was true and what wasn't when it came to what mother would say.

Joni said I should also try to help mother by getting her some vitamins and get her to take them. They would make her feel better and give her more energy. I had, in fact, gotten her some vitamins a few months earlier and told mother these exact things.

Next, Joni got into my personal relationships. Of course I wanted to know about the one I was kind of involved with now, and was M.C. worth it, and was it going to work. She first said that the man I was with on my forty fifth birthday would be the one. She wasn't sure if it was M.C. or not. She said, "There will be one that makes you laugh." I had told everyone that he could make me laugh. She continued, "If the one you are with now is the one, and I wanted it to work, there would be three critical issues." One would involve my pride. She said we would almost break up over that crisis. I felt like this had already happened, and I decided to give him another chance. "You will have to give up something." I had -- my pride by staying with him after finding out he was a cheater. "He may have to give up something with the second crises, and you both might have to within the third one." She continued with, "It was not going to be easy but if I wanted it to work it would." I wasn't sure at that point if he was even worth the effort or not. She took my other hand, "You are highly intelligent, but you haven't had enough education and you should keep up with current computer skills."

She also saw a trip coming that I should take, "on the shore with tall pine like trees." I should contemplate there she said. I didn't know pine like trees grew near the shore. "You are very psychic yourself and intuitive. You should pay more attention," she said. "There is a part of you that is silent that just observes and collects insight and you are able to understand people."

She ended with telling me I would have grandchildren, maybe twins. I told her grandkids would be great, but maybe not twins. Finally she said, "Success would come in my fifties." I wasn't too thrilled about this but declared, "Well, it's not that far off when you think about it." She couldn't believe I had a twenty-one year old daughter and that I was forty-three. She thought I would have about an eight year old. I laughed and thanked her for the compliment.

"Well, was any of that true? Did any of those things come about?"

Oh, you know when someone is telling you your fortune you are going over the events of the moment and think they are lining up. It's bull to me, but she did hit on some very close similarities as to what was going on, and of course she was spot on about me being intelligent and intuitive I must say. But as far as being with this guy or another or making it work, that was all a bunch of crap and I knew it would be, but I was curious.

The relationship with M.C. was all wrong and bad for me, but I got back with him. We bought a race car for him so he could race locally, and we opened a mechanic shop in the small town of Noble, south of Norman. He was full time National Guard, so I ran the shop during the day and he would come down after five. We had a mechanic that would work at night and part time mechanics during the day.

What went on for the next four and a half years was me working at the shop, and at one time during the winter months I even worked till midnight at Walmart as a cashier because we needed the money. M.C. was supposed to run the shop for a few hours after he got off work, but he didn't, so I quit working till midnight. He enjoyed tinkering with his race car, racing on the weekends, rearranging his tools and cheating. We split up for good. I let him have the car, trailer and whatever tools he wanted. Of course, he took the best ones which I had to replace in order to try to keep the mechanic shop going.

My mother called me one night at the shop and wanted me to go see her. I knew she only wanted me to buy her a bottle. I was not in the mood to deal with it or do whatever she wanted. I was tired, so I didn't go see her. I didn't go for a few days to see her and all seemed quiet. Fred's woman, Kandy, called to tell me she had been to see mother and thought she had had a stroke. I went to see her and discovered that, yes, she probably had. She didn't live alone, both Fred and Eldon lived with her. Later I confronted them "How could you not know?" After all they had to have been taking her to the bathroom and bed, etc., because she couldn't walk or use her left arm! I assume they were just so ignorant or maybe they thought she was extremely drunk. I don't know.

So I talked to her about the possibility that she had a stroke. She didn't believe me and was a bit defiant about it also. I went back to my mechanic shop and called a home health business. They told me that they would go check on her, and that a person hardly ever believes a family member of their misfortune. They are more apt to believe a professional.

Of course, she had indeed had a stroke. I don't remember who, how or the order of how she was taken to the hospital. I do remember a short-lived time in the hospital and some physical therapy. I also remember getting her into Jim Thorpe, one of the best physical therapy places in Oklahoma City. She hated it. She wanted out; no ifs ands or buts!

So, she didn't get all the therapy she could have received. They continued with some at home, but she would never really walk well again. She got around for some time using a walker. She complained about not being able to clean the house. I told her she could do some things. She could dust by getting around and sitting near the tables, etc., and dust. No, I guess she wasn't going to do that either. Anyway then about a year or so later, she broke a hip. That was pretty much the end of her walking all together. She had use of her arm but her poor beautiful left hand decided to kind of curl at the fingers. She complained that they did something wrong when they repaired her hip with a metal implant. It always hurt. She might have walked some with the walker after the hip replacement, but not long. Therapists worked with her for quite some time, but I guess she didn't care to get better. Not sure.

I say if she had had the stroke on the other side and it affected her speech, she would have died. After the stroke she could only demand, bitch and gripe from her throne, the recliner and you could always walk away. She couldn't follow, at least without some effort on her part. You still had ample time to get away from her mouth.

Her mouth would make me angry but if she poked me as she spoke as she did one Thanksgiving Day, I could come unglued. I had gone to her house to help her because Eldon's brother, the preacher, and his wife were coming for Thanksgiving

Dinner. Mother was already drinking early that day so she was mouthy and in everyone's faces. I was hurrying because I knew I was not going to stay because of her drinking. She got in my face about something and began poking me. That did it! I went for her throat and backed her up into her bedroom. She started to go down backwards onto the floor, but somehow I managed to help her down so that she wouldn't get hurt. I was still above her and continued to kind of choke her to shut her up. Teresa didn't know what to do. She put some tissue in mother's mouth because it was still going. She tried to spit it out and, believe it or not, even though my hands were around her throat, it bothered me that Teresa had tried to shut her up by putting tissue in her mouth. It might not sound comical, but it was in a way. I got up, gathered my things, my daughter and I left and never spent another holiday with her again.

I remember, Stacy this home health evaluator, talking to me on the phone once. She said, "I always wondered what you girls (sister and I) were talking about. Well, this morning I saw it!" Your mother was always very sweet, but this morning she let me have it!" I was almost laughing when I said loudly, "Yeah, it's her mouth! It's her mouth!"

Regardless of her mouth, her sometimes hatefulness, her criticisms, her dislike for dogs and little children, everyone loved her, including me. Yes, as rotten as she was to me, as critical, as unloving, as demanding, as cruel, We all loved her. I don't understand it, but everyone loved her. Even dogs would go up to her and babies wanted her attention. What is that? I thought perhaps the dogs and little children were a punishment -- that as much as they annoyed her, that's what she got -- annoyance and punishment.

Most of the visitors to she and Eldon's house were, of course, people that were accustomed to drinking and or doing drugs. Most were my brothers' friends that they grew up with and some were Eldon's druggy friends. Mother drank with them and wanted to argue about religion and politics. I would never argue any subject with her ever because I didn't stay around when she was drinking. I hated her when she drank, and I didn't think she knew very much about what she wanted to argue about. "Even when I'm wrong, I'm right!" she would say. How do you argue with that? But those that drank with her amused her and therefore got her moving on to the next day. She would even cut them down to their faces and they still loved her and came back for more.

Mother and Eldon never married either, but they were together about twenty six years I believe. She and Eldon got a divorce a few years after she broke her hip, but he still went to check on her even though he had moved in with a woman who had some emotional issues. He was in the same mobile home park a few streets away. My mother loved it out there. It was kind of in the country. She said it reminded her of when she was a little girl. When she was in the wheelchair for good, I would go visit and make sure she got outside to enjoy the fresh air. We would just sit out there and talk. Even though Fred was living with her, he didn't do much. He didn't drive so he couldn't take her to doctor appointments. She had home health come in to bathe her, make sure she was taking meds, and they also were to do some cleaning in the house. Fred did cook and clean some.

Although I was always the one to take care of everything for the family especially after they would all get in a mess, I now became the child who took over the elder care responsibilities as well. "You're the only one who has any sense." One compliment she gave me throughout the years, and she was right. Oh wow, she was right once in a while.

"Where was your sister? Why wasn't she helping?"

Teresa and I have always been close. We know and trust each other completely and love each other very much. She loved Mother too, and she would have helped if she was able. Unfortunately, she got hooked on pain pills in the early nineties due to a very bad leg injury, and it took her many years to get better.

Eldon told Mother she wouldn't live more than a year after breaking her hip. I guess he said statistics show or something like that. She lived about eight years. She could get up from bed into her wheelchair, piddle around and get into her recliner. She wouldn't go outside on her own, even though there was a ramp built for her. Perhaps she was afraid to go out on her own. I tried to tell her once she finally agreed to a battery operated chair, to go up to the mailboxes or go visit a friend a few doors away, but she never did. Even though Fred was there, he wasn't really there she said. "He doesn't do anything. He's no company to me." Still though, there must have been some comfort in the fact that she was not in a house all by herself, especially as an invalid. I hated that the last eight years of her life became even more debilitating and miserable for her. She still had her mouth though...she still had her mouth.

CHAPTER TWENTY

I closed the shop a few months after M.C. and I split because I had no income other than what the shop was making, and it didn't make much. I stayed with my daughter for a short time and got a job in Oklahoma City at a parts recycling business. It employed many interesting folks. One day they wanted me to train some people. They brought what I thought was a sixteen year old, little black girl for me to train. Her name was Gwen. She was actually in her early forties, and she was the hardest working person I'd ever known, besides me. We became friends. She was raising one of her grandsons who happened to be the same age as my granddaughter. I had mentioned to her about my granddaughter talking about Jude who was this spirit that she could see. She didn't really talk about him, but would say his name and point for the longest because she really didn't say much until about three to four years old. It really freaked me out, especially when she pointed out a costume in Walmart of a ghost and said, "Jude," or when she was a little older and told me he holds her and his arm was gross.

Gwen said that her grandson talked about DaDa. (pronounced with long a's) That was his spirit. I told Gwen, "We have to tell them to leave. Demand they leave in the name of Jesus." For which we did.

I understood this seeing of spirits because one night when I was about five, I had gone to the kitchen to get a drink of milk, and I saw a little man standing by the refrigerator. He was about three feet tall and wore a coat and hat like the character Dick Tracy. It scared me really badly, and I ran back to my bed and covered up my head. So remembering this one day, I drew a picture of my ghost and asked my almost two year old granddaughter, "Jude?" She said "No," and then I drew a picture of a Casper like ghost. Her eyes widened, she pointed at it and said, "Jude."

One day my daughter and granddaughter were at the mechanic shop with me. My daughter said she thought they ought to be heading home, and I saw my granddaughter's eyes follow something from the corner of the ceiling and out the door as if Jude flew out quickly to get in the van and catch a ride home with them.

When I still owned the mechanic shop, I was telling a parts delivery woman about my granddaughter's ghost. She began to tell me about her daughter's little imaginary friend or so they thought. She said her daughter would talk to and about her imaginary friend all the time. One day she heard her husband let out a horrifying scream, and when she ran into the living room he told her he saw a little man that looked like Dick Tracy run across the room. I got chills. I couldn't believe he may have seen the same little creature that I had seen so many years ago. I told her about my Dick Tracy, and she confirmed that the overcoat and hat was why he said it looked like Tracy.

"Not everyone is open to such phenomenon."

I know. But my girls are. When my daughter was two, she would talk about her other mother and her brother and how he burned up in their house. Two! One time she was talking about her mother, and I said something like, "I didn't do that," and she replied with, "Not you, my other mother."

Also when she was about three to four, she would be crying in her room in the middle of the night. I would find her huddled down on the floor, terrified of something. I would comfort her before putting her back to bed. I wasn't sure what these were, but they sounded like night terrors and not too uncommon, possibly being brought on by being overtired. This was better than the other thing that I had heard about -- children seeing black creature spirits in the night coming after them.

Also when my daughter was four and a half, I went to a Halloween party dressed as a wolf. Seems like my mother was babysitting and I went home to check on her with my full costume on. When she saw me she started to back up and began saying some kind of chant. It sounded like a record being played backwards. I was pretty scared, so I ripped my mask off and said, "It's Mommy, it's Mommy!" I didn't want her putting some kind of hex on me or cause me to burst into flames. I got down on my knees and hugged her, feeling bad that I had scared her so badly that some inner ancient hex, curse or spell was shooting out of her mouth.

Now you tell me there aren't spirits in our world. I've heard that a young mind, open and fresh, can see such things. Still something else I read was that because children have just passed over into this world, these ghosts or spirits they see are actually relatives that are acting as guardians until they feel the child no longer needs one. I've also heard that there is a spirit world that runs parallel to our world. I guess we will have all the answers when we enter heaven.

"Did you ever see anything else yourself?"

No, can't say that I did. I do remember when I was a teenager and had to do all that lifting, it felt like someone had helped me on the other end of my load a couple of times. Also I did experience once when I was pretty depressed the feeling that I knew everything. My sister said she experienced this once and I heard of one other person who thought they knew everything.

"I don't understand."

Well, it was like for a few minutes, I felt I had the answers to everything in life. I knew everything and it felt good and very satisfying. I felt like everything was not that big of a deal, and I was so content that I felt like it would be okay to just die then.

"Don't believe I have ever heard of this."

I have only heard of the three of us. I tried looking it up on the internet, but couldn't find anything referencing anything quite like this either.

"So you moved in with your daughter?"

No. I stayed with her for a couple of weeks. I think she and her husband thought I was going to stay there forever. I didn't feel comfortable, so I got that data entry position at the parts recycling place in one day and left as soon as I could. I actually stayed with my good friends, Bob and Sheila. Even though the drive to and from work was much further from their house than my daughter's, I felt more welcome and comfortable. It seems like I stayed with them for a month or two until I found an apartment I could afford.

"Were you seeing anyone?"

Not really. I think I was kind of seeing this one guy named John who was unemployed at the time, but it wasn't anything serious -- more like friends. It took me awhile to figure out what his issues may have been.

John had a great mind. He came from a good family. They owned a pharmacy. He was a geologist and had played baseball at the University of Oklahoma. His career had taken him to many parts of the world. He had an ex-wife and a son. He was applying for jobs in different parts of the world when we met. I kept assuring him that he would get one soon. He wanted me to go with him to Cape Cod, South America or even Bahrain. He said these were the areas that he was liable to get a job. I could just see me going off, God knows where, and then hating this man and being stuck. One thing I hate is the feeling of being stuck, constricted in some way. That's why I have always had and kept options.

"Would you hate him?"

Trust me; I would have grown to hate him as I did with most of my men. Well, first of all I didn't even know him that well or had not even felt that attracted to him. He seemed more like a friend that I didn't know very well. I just let him talk about taking me. I thought about it. I might have gone just to get away from the family. I always wanted to get away from the family.

"Do you think that is why you dated so many foreign men?"

Perhaps, who knows, maybe to get as far away as possible from them. Well, Mother mainly, I guess. Or was it just that I craved something more exciting out of life? Not more drama or turmoil -- just something different and exciting.

Anyway, I was friends with John and another man named Glenn, who was a very nice military man who didn't talk much. I kind of liked that because I used to think that men didn't have much to say that was worth anything, or I didn't care what they had to say. I thought they should have just been there for whatever you wanted and then put them away in a closet. I wish it were that easy.

Did I mention I had put an ad on Match.com?

"I don't think you did. I don't understand. If you didn't like men why continue to date and look?"

I can't really explain. I had no respect for them. I hated them but wanted one. I wanted one to love me and take care of me as portrayed in some movies or soaps or from what I had observed in the world. I mean people got married and had children and homes and social lives, maybe I wanted that. Maybe I just didn't know how to achieve those things because I kept picking the wrong men. Maybe I was afraid of that kind of life. Perhaps I thought I would get bored with a comfortable life. Maybe I was afraid I wouldn't have what freedom I had or I wouldn't be allowed to pursue my dreams. I had no example of such a life really. Even when my father was alive, even though it was pretty normal, it wasn't for me because of my mother's treatment of me. That was the best time though, before my father's death. It only got worse after that.

There were many men interested in me but I wasn't in them; however, not too long after I had put this ad up, I got a reply from a man asking. "What do you have in mind?" Now the ad said I was looking for a long term commitment and or marriage. I thought, "What?" and sat on it for a few days. Finally I responded about what I had in mind. From there he emailed, "I was visiting family in northeast Oklahoma and looking at the Tulsa World." I don't even remember how that got him looking at the ads, but I accepted whatever he said, and we began talking. I was forty-nine, he fifty-nine.

His name was Morris, a car salesman from California. I loved his humor, his voice and his charm.

"And the fact that he was from California probably didn't hurt either. And, considerably older than you were used to."

Yes, I loved California and I was a bit concerned about his age but, hell, I had tried almost everything else. So we started to talk and get acquainted. He said he moved to California with his family as a child -- originally a country boy from the northeast part of Oklahoma. He talked about how he got into a lot of fights with the California boys and that he was pretty big and could hurt them pretty badly. His parents sent him off to a camp which he enjoyed very much and later on as a teen, he skipped school to surf. He said he joined the Navy and became a seal during the Vietnam War.

He had been married twice, but then there was another woman in there that he married out of convenience and helped raise her daughter. He had two children by his first wife who, by the way, was the original Rosie of "Rosie and the Originals," a famous singing group in the fifties. His second marriage was with a much younger woman and they had a son. They were divorced, and therefore he was looking for a friend.

After a couple of months he wanted to meet me in person, sent me a plane ticket and said "Look for the tall, good looking man holding a rose and looking nervous."

I think it was summer 2001. I was a bit excited to go and not afraid. I got to the ticket counter and found out that my driver's license was expired by two months. "If it were any other airline," the ticket seller said, "You would not be able to get on the plane." I was, however, instructed to go down the hall and get scanned and patted down before I was allowed to board the plane.

This was the beginning of our seven to eight year relationship. Most of it was long distance, but it worked for me for a quite a while. After all, Mother was ill, and even though I would have loved to run away, I just couldn't leave her when she was pretty much an invalid and so dependent on me.

During this time I was getting a bit tired of working in Oklahoma City. I saw a business from the highway in Norman. I wasn't sure what it was exactly but I said, "Someday I'm going to work there." I kept looking at that place every morning that I drove forty-five minutes to work in the City and I looked at it every evening on my way home. The sign read, Metro Turf and I noticed there were riding mowers on display in the yard.

One day there was an ad in the paper for a service manager. I called. Metro Turf was a lawn equipment sales and service business. I felt confident I could do it. After all, I had experience as a service manager from my mechanic shop. In the interview I realized these two brothers, the owners, were Persian, so I mentioned being married to one many years ago and threw out David's name in case they knew him and could get some brownie points. They didn't know him. I was hired.

"You realize that when you make such claims, such as when you were going to film your movie at that brush arbor, that they did come true?"

Should do it more often -- must be the result of positive thinking.

The Astanis, owners of Metro Turf in Norman, were not Muslim. They were of the Baha'i religion. Another religious group besides the Jews that were persecuted by the Muslims in Iran. They seemed to be very nice men and very respectful to me. We happened to have some friends in common. I met a woman named Jill who worked there, and we became friends even though she said I was such a bitch when I would say, "What was that?" when she coughed so badly because of her smoking. Even though she was kind of joking about calling me a bitch, my response to her cough actually helped her to quit smoking. I was so proud of her for sticking to it. I had never known anyone that quit smoking. Then she went on a diet and she stuck with that, too, and did very well. She must have a strong constitution.

I loved the job, but about two months into the job, I slipped on some grease in the shop area and fell right on my behind, hard. I cleaned up the grease and told one of my bosses about it. A couple of days later I started to have some pain in my lower back, and I felt like I was walking funny. My friend Lisa noticed it one night when we went to her son's baseball game. She recommend that I go to her chiropractor and get checked out. I did, and they began to work on me, but it didn't seem to be helping much.

Because of my age and due to the fact that this was my second back injury over the years, I decided to get a lawyer and file a claim with workman's comp. The first injury to my back was when I worked for the University, but it was higher up, just below my shoulder blades and in the middle. Somehow I hurt it moving file cabinets. I went to therapy for a few months and had some cortisone shots in my back. They also said I had some bone spurs in that area. Somehow, as I talked with the therapists, we figured out that I had lifted too much as a child and teen when my back was not fully developed therefore causing spurs and arthritis in that area. One day I told my mother about this to make her feel bad but it didn't seem to work.

I told the chiropractor that he wasn't helping me, and he thought I should see a neurologist. I saw one -- was offered pain pills which I refused. He sent me for physical therapy. I continued to work every day through the pain and therapy.

Morris and I continued our phone relationship, and occasionally I would talk to John and Glenn. However, you know you are in trouble when you have to call one of your best friends to come and take your gun from your home.

"Just keep it for a while till I get better." I laughed, but I didn't find it funny. I didn't want Sheila to know how really tired I was of my life, again. I had been into my eighth month of physical therapy for the back injury. At some point, calls from Morris had become almost nil. His calls became less in April, then one call in May. I didn't know what was going on with him. I missed him; and, I missed his humor. At least he made me laugh.

I was tired of the physical pain and now emotional pain and depression. Work, therapy, home. Work, therapy, home. Then there was the responsibilities I had for my mother and I was the only one she could count on to do anything. Nothing new about that, but it's harder to deal with things when in pain.

This was all I was doing and it was slowly beating me down. I had also gained more weight since my injury and didn't need to do that. I needed to lose several pounds -- not gain.

I had a regiment of stretches and exercises to do twice a day to strengthen the muscles in my back. I just wanted to be strong, healthy and in love, and I was so tired of working. Nothing was going my way. I prayed. What else could I do? I was grateful for a job that I liked, even though with my back it was very hard for me. I was in constant pain. I thanked God almost daily for the job that kept me in my apartment, allowed me to pay my bills, buy groceries and drive a vehicle. But that is all God had given me. Just enough. Nothing extra for Georgianne.

Morris would usually call every day when going to work and then again when going home -- rarely ever in between. I could almost set my clock to his calls. There would be those times though when he wouldn't call for a few days.

One time when Morris had not called for a couple of weeks I called John. He had some health issues at the time, still living with his mother helping her and still applying for jobs all over the world.

I had gone to dinner with John previously so still in contact with him. It was perfectly innocent. As if it mattered. Had I known the type of man Morris was, perhaps I would have had other men friends. Wait, I did, but I never had sex with them while I was with Morris.

"You were faithful to Morris even though it was a shaky deal and long distance?"

Yes. I know -- crazy. My sister told me I needed to see other men, local men, but oh no, I was stuck on this guy like no other.

It was as if Morris had someone watching me or really good radar. The night I went out to dinner with John, Morris called. Another time John was at my house doing some research on my computer and Morris called. John was over another evening, watching a movie and Morris called. I didn't answer his calls. I couldn't talk to him then -- he would have known I wasn't alone. It made me think that God was telling me to wait for Morris. I know that's stupid because I had been through these kinds of stupid thoughts before with each of my men.

"Signals from God?"

I know it sounds stupid and childish but I had pretty much lived my life like that. After all, what did I know about anything? I'm still not sure if it was God or Satan guiding me.

"What do you mean?"

Well, had I not done certain things such as staying with each relationship until I could no longer take anymore abuse and unhappiness, would I have traveled the paths that I needed to, in order to learn the things I needed to learn in this life? Would I have been able to help my mother and her children live had I gone away from them? Would I have met all the wonderful people I have met in my life or turned out to be the kind of person I am today? And who knows, maybe someone learned something from knowing me.

I know the choices were mine, but who was guiding me or putting things or people in my paths?

Back to when I hadn't heard from Morris for a little over two weeks. I decided that was it; tired of him taking me for granted. I called John and he invited me over. He did need a ride to the store for a few groceries. He had been in the hospital, something to do with some blockage to his heart, so he said he couldn't drive. There were other times when I invited him to my place or some function before I had met Morris, but he either couldn't get there or just didn't show up. I found out in the end, it was because John was actually an alcoholic and possibly a prescription drug addict, and I think his license may have been suspended.

On my way to his house that night which was probably about 40 miles away, Morris called. I hadn't heard from him for over two weeks and he calls when I am driving to John's. I had even planned on spending the night for company. Morris's radar was up. I talked to him as I drove. He had a story that one might find hard to believe, but so unusual maybe it was true. He said he had been working on his daughter's lake home, outside laying bricks for a patio when he got stung by a scorpion. Now he said he had gone to the doctor and they told him to watch it. The bite was on his leg. He didn't think much of it and thought he was watching it, but he said one day he took his sock off and found his leg swollen and green stuff coming out of his toe! The scorpion had stung him on his leg that they had taken an artery from for his bypass surgery when he was fifty -- right on the spot. He continued to tell me that he ended up in a hyperbaric chamber. He said he didn't call because they thought he might lose his leg and he had poison all through his system. He didn't want me to worry.

I did go to John's house that night. Visited with him and his mother. Took John to the store, ate dinner with them and then watched a movie with him. All I could think of as I watched the movie was, "I need to get home and call Morris." I felt as if I was doing something wrong -- as if I was being unfaithful. I did not spend the night. I drove home late that night and called 'manipulative' Morris when I got home.

Several months later, I was home watching a movie waiting for Morris to call when I felt I should call John. His mother had died a few days before and her funeral was this day. I had talked to him earlier that week, but should have called him that night. The next morning I was watching the news. I saw and heard a story that I couldn't believe and thought it was on the street where John lived. I saw his house and couldn't believe what had happened.

"What happened?"

Well, apparently he and family members had attended his mother's funeral. He probably started drinking and taking something when he got home. Some family members were calling and harassing him about what, I have no clue. I heard that John called 911 and told them what was going on and that if any of the family showed up that the police would have to bring body bags.

As the evening went on, I guess it got worse. A woman cop was sent to his home and he shot at the door from inside. Missed her but hit his car in the driveway. When that happened and they found out his fourteen year old son was in the house, they considered it a hostage situation and sent more police. At some point John walked out onto the front porch with gun in hand, raised to fire. It jammed and they shot him dead center in the forehead.

"Oh my. Was his son all right?"

Yes, he was fine. I learned about all of this from his son. In fact, his son said he was never in danger, wasn't worried or scared. In fact he said he was just in his room listening to music. He definitely wasn't afraid of his dad -- ever. I think he was just out of his mind that night with the help of booze and narcotics. It was very sad. He was very kind, caring and had a brilliant mind.

"I am surprised you had him for a friend."

Oh, because of the chemical abuse? I didn't know about it for quite a while. Like I said, he had excuses for not joining me on occasions. Whenever I did see him, he was straight. Yes, I would never knowingly get involved with anyone, male or female, who was an alcoholic or drug abuser. I had enough of that in my immediate family.

When I told Morris he said, "Good." I guess he thought John was a threat to our relationship, but he wasn't at all. In fact, when I figured out John's problem, well that just killed any chance he had with me.

So Morris and I continued on. He had sold his house and was living on his large sailboat in San Diego Bay area for which I was invited to visit. That was fun. In fact, Morris and I had a lot of fun together, whether here in Oklahoma or in California. He was a fun guy -- a guy who loved life.

Another time Morris quit calling about the time he was about to move to Oklahoma. He had bought a home. He showed me the pictures the last time I was in California. I figured his move to Oklahoma was just too close for comfort. He said he was moving back because he grew up in Oklahoma and now was ready for a simpler, quieter life. He may have gotten scared, I thought. Maybe he thought I would demand a real commitment now that he was so close. I didn't know at the time. You never really know what is in someone's mind. I found out later why he hadn't called. I found out later, how manipulative he was. How I never had a clue. He was very charismatic and knew just how to keep me interested in him.

"Was your back getting better?"

Not really. The physical therapy didn't seem to be helping. They had even put me on a stretcher table. That only hurt worse. They tried everything. I went back to the neurologist. He sent me to a doctor who gave me steroid shots in the muscles of my lower back, and then they tried three epidurals that didn't seem to help.

"How long had this been going on? You must have been in a lot of pain and you didn't take pain pills?"

About the fifteenth month one of the doctors sent me to another physical therapy place. The man was magnificent. He had me lay on a table and he gently touched my vertebrae all the way down. He said, "Your sacrum is hanging down. Most times it will be tilted but yours is hanging down, and all the therapy you have been doing has only been aggravating it." He gently put it in place. I had another three months of gentle therapy with him and was released.

"So your back is good now?"

Oh no. I have constant pain in my upper back from hard work, and the first injury and the lower back has pain whenever it feels like it. I regularly go to a chiropractor to keep me in line, and I feel to keep me walking straight.

"Still no pain pills?"

No. I have never had a pain pill in my life, not even when I had my bottom wisdom teeth pulled in my forties and ended up looking like a chipmunk for several days.

"Are you afraid you would get hooked on them?"

Not exactly. I don't have addictive behavior nor does my daughter like the rest of my family. I am more afraid of how my body would react to such meds. It seems like my body overreacts to stimulants.

"I see."

You know after the incident with David and my daughter, I went to a psychiatrist and they wanted to put me on something, but I refused – in fact I didn't go back. My friend Vinnie has always thought I should be on Prozac or something like that, but I have refused. I never ever wanted to alter my mind, feelings or judgment. God would help me get through anything that came my way. I had a lot of faith in God and in myself even though I've had times of weakness.

So eventually Morris moved to that house in Oklahoma. He came to see me in Norman many times, about three hours to the west, but I wasn't invited to his place. He had allowed two of his cousins to live there while he was still in California, and they were still living there with him. They were sisters. I kept telling him that was weird and that they needed to move out. One of them did move, but the other stayed on for probably another year or so.

I did go over a couple of times when the one cousin, Dorothy, still lived there. Once she moved out, my visits were more often. Still there was no more of a commitment between Morris and me though.

CHAPTER TWENTY-ONE

I didn't go to many parades as an adult, probably didn't go to too many as a child for that matter. But one time I went to a Christmas parade in Norman with my friend Mary -- Mary, the kind of sweet, caring woman who could always fill you with words that would make you feel better about yourself. The year was 2005. It was sunny and quite cool. It was an all right parade, I assume. Don't remember much of it until about the last float when I heard this music and saw this young, beautiful girl singing. What a wonderful voice she had.

"Wow, I wonder who she is?" Mary commented that she somehow knew who she was and that started the ball rolling. Her name was Allison Mullins. I don't remember all the details on how I got to meet her and talk with her, but I remember going to hear her sing a few times. I thought she was really good.

Years previously I had written some lyrics and had music set to them from a company in Nashville. I thought I could help her in some way -- didn't know how at the time. Perhaps she would sing some of my songs and maybe we could write some together.

Several years before I had tried to do this with a male singer. I even tried to manage another young man, but he and his wife moved away.

Since I had known Alice, Reba's sister, I had written to her and mentioned something about Allison. At that time Alice was not doing anything with singers, and gave me her daughter's address and phone number. She thought her daughter might be able to help me even though some years previously we had talked about my CD, but she was out of the business then.

Her daughter and I had talked. I remember her asking me if she was as good a singer or along the same lines as LeAnn

Rimes. I told her "Yes." She allowed me to send her a CD but she was promising nothing.

Allison had already produced a couple of CD's, so I sent one to Alice's daughter. I offered to help with some financing on her next CD. I also asked her if she would put a song or two of mine on her new CD. Nothing came of either endeavors, and I quit trying to be a bother to everyone.

Time went by. I had seen Allison sing a few times as I said, and she did sing one of my songs a time or two. She graduated from high school a couple years after I had first seen her on that float. She had been making trips with her grandmother to Texas, Colorado, or wherever else they were having American Idol tryouts. She never got picked to be on the show, so she continued to work at her grandmother's scrapbook store and singing where and when she could.

One day I stopped by the scrapbook store. Allison told me she was going to move to Nashville. I was sad but also excited for her. Oh, to be so young and ambitious and ready to just leap into an adventure like that. I wrote her a check for a couple hundred dollars or so. It was not much, but I had wanted to give her that for graduation -- not for leaving, but as I said, I was happy for her, but would miss knowing she wasn't close.

"I'm sorry. Did she leave?'

No, she didn't. Something did not pan out. So Allison continued to sing locally everywhere she could. She also got a job as a Deejay at a radio station south of Norman.

We continued to talk about writing something together. Life went on as usual. I always felt like I wanted to help her in some way. Morris said his daughter may know someone in California that would be interested in her, so I gave him a copy of her CD. Nothing came of that either. I never gave her money for a CD as I didn't feel like I could part with a large amount of money most of the time. We continued to talk and text from then on.

"I find it remarkable that you continued to try to be creative through all the years and responsibilities that were thrust

upon you."

"How was the situation with Fred and your mother at this time?"

Well, Fred was in his own hell. He was an alcoholic, he did drugs and he had become a cutter. I didn't care about him much. He was worthless and, as he said to me once, "You've hated me since I touched your daughter." Exactly. I didn't really talk to him after the age of 11 since that happened. I truly believe that the evil spirit that was in Buss passed into Fred when Buss died. I think Fred battled good and evil for the rest of his life. He was mostly good, but he had to be dealing with some demons. One day he looked at me, and for a moment I saw the evil in his face and it looked just as his father. I wanted to love him, but I didn't like the way he was.

Just as I never really talked to Fred, I never really talked to Eldon. If you put all of my words that came out of my mouth to say something to Eldon in about the 33 years that we had all known him, I bet it was no more than 2 hours, if that. I hated him. Did not like him from the time Mother met him.

So there came a time when the manager at the mobile home park Mother and Fred were living at found out Fred was living there. They had ousted him once and threatened to evict Mother if he showed up again. He was caught looking in someone's window once and they turned him in. He said he looked in because they didn't answer the door and he just wanted to see if they were ignoring him. They were thugs and doing drugs. He wanted some. That's what he claimed. Probably the truth. Anyway, so he laid low for a very long time, and for a very long time the management never knew he lived there. They sent her an eviction notice because she had broken the rules. Rules, Mother, there are rules for reasons. She never went by the rules and she sure wasn't going to toss her worthless son out.

I told him he had to leave long before that and now time was up. I don't remember why I went to my Mother's one night. I think she needed something. She was in bed and I did whatever it was she needed. Maybe it was because I was mad at Fred for the eviction notice or something but for some reason he and I got into it. Now mind you, I was 53, he was 40. We exchanged words and I roughed him up. All I could think of was how I wanted to toss him out of the big window in his room -- and I could have, too. He kept backing down as I pushed him into a chair, but he kept getting up for more and I gave it to him. He got up three times and I knocked him down three times. Who knows what was going on in his head? I felt I needed to get out of there or kill him. I went back to check on Mother again, and she asked me what was going on. I told her, "If I don't get out of here right now, I'll kill him."

The next day I heard through Mother's home health administrator that Fred was going to press charges on me if I showed up again. I didn't give a rat's ass, but I said, "You know what? Who cares? Let him deal with Mom and where they are going and what they are going to do." In a way, it was a good thing for me to not care, to be fed up enough to just let it go, but a terrible thing to do to them because it all turned out bad in the end.

The mobile home was Mother's and paid for. It was an older home and in need of some repairs, but she could have lived there till she died. She could have died in her home instead of a nursing home had she kicked Fred out, had she asked him to leave or made him leave since he wasn't man enough to go on his own for the good of his Mother. Instead, just like his father, he ruined what she had left -- her home.

I heard that Fred had the mobile home moved. He was moving it out to a town even further south out in the country where someone he knew lived on five acres. I heard the mobile home's tongue broke, I believe that's what it's called -- the apparatus in the front of the mobile home that connects to the truck then to be hauled. So, this big mobile home was in a church parking lot on a highway south of where they lived.

My mother, an elderly invalid mind you now, stayed at my sister's for several days or a week or two while they figured out how to get this thing welded and out to this what I found out later was actually a mobile home cemetery, except the man Fred knew had a nice home out there. Somehow, without me, Fred managed to get the mobile home moved out there and somehow even the ramp got taken out to the new location. However, there was no electricity connected. I am not even sure how the water was connected or if it even was. I remember the home health people telling me that they did not have electricity on, but they had an extension cord going to this guy's house. When it became apparent that it was unfit for my mother to be there, they called me.

Now it's not that I didn't try to help my mother in the past. I got a place for her and my sister once so they could help each other. It was in a nice apartment on the west side of town. Problem with this was timing. Teresa was going with a worthless person and very depressed. So if she had good intentions to make a nice home for them, it just couldn't happen. My mother barely got out of the bedroom. I would come and get her and take her for a ride, go to Sonic or get a Schlotzsky's sandwich and take her to the park to eat. Sometimes I would just wheel her out to the courtyard and visit with her.

One day I went over there and my sister's worthless boyfriend was asleep on the couch. The house was a mess. Teresa was lying on the floor next to Mother's bed, which she did often to be near her. They apparently watched many movies at night that way. I am glad Teresa had that time with her. Anyway, there was also a couple sleeping in the other bedroom. It was probably around noon. I lost it. I threw some clothes at the boyfriend and yelled, "Get a job." I went to the bedroom, opened the door and yelled the same thing. I went back into the living room where the boyfriend was up without a shirt and hiking at his jeans and acting as if he wanted to fight. He was a scrawny fella, but he had muscles. I wish he had come at me. I was mad enough, I thought I could take him. If not, well I would have fought like hell or I would have gone for a knife, who knows. He didn't make his move as I yelled at him. I went back into Mom's bedroom and told her I had to get out of there before I killed somebody.

Another night I had gone over to check on Mother. It was the day before Thanksgiving and Teresa had good intentions to make a turkey. I can't remember what was going on, but Mother wanted to go home to her mobile home where Fred was living -- out there where there was no electricity and possibly no running water. I had tried to make things better but it wasn't working out. Mother and I got into it about her wanting to leave and go out there regardless. I wanted her to be in a better place. She just wanted to be stupid as usual. How could she want to go out there and why? I finally called Fred and yelled, "Come and get her!" I used to yell a lot and had a very bad temper.

"So much stress. And sometimes you just can't help those who don't want it. You say there was another time?"

Yes, but here again, when the home health services found out Mother went back to her mobile home in the country with no working electricity, they ended up putting her in a nursing home. There were many elderly people at the nursing home, but it seemed as if there were more with mental issues. Mother must have been there for a couple of months. Then my sister found this really cute house and assured me that if I could arrange to get it, she would take care of Mom again. She was single, had gotten rid of her boyfriend and I thought we should try. None of us wanted her in a nursing home. I paid the deposit and first and last month's rent as required. It soon got cluttered. My sister wasn't doing well there either. I think that only lasted about three months. Mother got sick and ended up in the hospital. She was pretty bad off. I didn't think she was going to get out of there alive, something to do with her stomach. She was in ICU and we had to wear those paper garments and masks to visit her. She had what they called C-diff (Clostridium Difficile); an overgrowth of bad organisms in the intestinal tract.

When she got out of ICU and into a room, at some point they wanted to put a feeding tube in her, but she refused. I asked them also at some point if they thought she had cancer. They told me they didn't know and she wouldn't let them do any kind of tests.

I stayed with her day and night for a few days. There was an awful ice storm, and I called into work one morning to check in and was told that they needed me. I didn't understand why with the ice storm. It was a lawn mower sales and service business. I was the service manager and also filed all the warranties, why did they need me?

I said, "We only have so many chainsaws or chains to sell." There were many trees down. They replied, "No, we got a shipment in and have many to sell, and customers are lined up. We need your help."

I told Mother I had to leave for a while. I know she didn't want to be alone. I think she thought she was going to die soon. She asked if I would call Eldon's girlfriend, of all people, to come to the hospital and stay with her till I got back or as long as she could. Eldon's girlfriend, the little bit off lady, surprisingly she and Mother were friendly toward each other. I know my mother was desperate to have wanted that woman to sit with her.

Electricity was out throughout the city of Norman because of that 2007 ice storm and I was afraid to drive on the ice, but others had done it and they needed me badly. I was a very loyal employee, made it there safely but with no shower, no fresh makeup and very little mascara, not to mention what little sleep I had had in the past few nights. I looked and felt awful. I pointed to my face and said to my boss, Mike, "This is what you get." He said I looked fine and thanked me for coming in.

I found out that Eldon's girlfriend didn't stay long that day nor did Eldon. I felt bad, but couldn't be in two places at once.

I took Mother a DVD made from our old family film movies that I managed to save from Buss tossing in the trash, for her to watch when she was feeling a bit better. I bought her a CD player and a CD of hymnal music so she could begin to be at peace. I thought her time to depart us was soon. Some months later, she said she didn't remember watching the DVD of the family with me. Oh well, at least, just as throughout my life, I tried to do everything I could for her. The old footage of us in a happier time when my dad was alive, I thought would make her happy. The CD player with earphones was to block out thoughts as well as noise of the hospital to bring her peace. She never could remember how to work it, but guarded that CD player as if knowing it was her last gift. Maybe she thought someone would take it or maybe it gave her comfort just knowing I gave it to her or at least that's what I like to think.

Surprisingly Mother got better, but by then there was not a home to go back to and she couldn't get back into the same nursing home that she had been in previously. They did not have a room for her. I called around and most nursing homes wouldn't take her in due to the C-diff. I called a man that was one of my customers when I owned the mechanic shop with M.C. He managed one of the Grace Living Centers in Norman. He said he would take her as soon as he had a room.

I had tried to get Mother to go to a Catholic Nursing Home in Oklahoma City once many years before this, but she wouldn't go. I thought it would be good for her to find peace with God for whatever had been tormenting her all these years. I wish she had gone, but you can't take an alcoholic too far from the booze, even though in her later years she didn't drink that much. She mostly would just have a beer on the table beside her chair. She would just sip on it off and on all day. If someone would visit her, they might bring something stronger and share with her, or she would have them go buy some liquor but it got to be less and less.

There were no rooms in the inn. I finally found a nursing home that could take her despite the infection. She hated it. She said "There are just old people here waiting to die." Now, my mother didn't have any friends her own age, well just one, Wilma, but she was a bit younger and lived in Vinita, three hours away. Mother liked young people, fun people and unlike the other nursing home, this place was full of old people and stricter rules for which she didn't like. It was depressing. I went to see her one day and they said she was in the cafeteria. I went down the hall to the area and looked toward the floor of tables. My eyes scanned the few people sitting scattered around, but I didn't see her. I finally located her. She was dressed, sitting with her head down resting it on her one good arm on the table. It hurt me to see her like that and I felt so bad for her.

What kind of daughter was I? Many times I thought about

taking her to my small apartment. It was only a one bedroom, but I wouldn't have minded to set her up in what was a dining area. I would have given her the bedroom, but she wouldn't have been able to get her wheelchair in and out of the door. The dining area was right there within the living room and tiny kitchen to the right. Home health could have come in every day. I could have taken care of her in the evening and during the night. I might not have gotten much sleep and I might have been worn out completely considering my job that was somewhat stressful and fast-paced and my back problems. I felt guilty, of course, but the main reason why I didn't take her in was because of my siblings, Eldon or any of their friends. I couldn't trust that they wouldn't come over. I didn't trust any of them and I couldn't trust that my brother, Fred, wouldn't come over, hang out or worse, steal from me. I didn't want to deal with any drama or drunks or pot heads. My sister said later trying to make me feel guilty, "I wouldn't have come over much or created a problem. Nobody would have come over." Really? Who was she trying to kid?

My place was my sanctuary, my safe haven. When I was within my walls, I could pick and choose who I let in. I could come and go as I pleased. I could ignore a phone call or a knock at the door and I didn't need to be invaded by all kinds of people. I could go to bed when I wanted, eat what I wanted, and clean my apartment or not. I could even take a nap if I wanted. With Mother in a nursing home -- safe, this, my feeling of aloneness, my feelings of not having to be responsible for everything, this feeling of some freedom was feeling pretty good.

I visited Mother at this new nursing home many times during the few weeks that she was there. She was not happy; she wanted to go back to the other nursing home. I knew why. The staff was young and fun, even some of the residents were young. Even though they may have had some mental issues, she enjoyed them. Many of the employees loved Mother and she befriended this one man named Terry who was probably fiftyish. He had some mental illness, I am not sure what was going on with him, but apparently they talked religion together and I knew how she loved that. So they had a friendship. Everyone called him her boyfriend. You know how that is in a nursing home. God bless him though.

I was constantly checking with the previous home. They wanted to take her back, but didn't have a room at the time. The director was actually a woman who, when she was a little girl, went to school with my daughter. I coached her in what was called something like Optimist Club Basketball when they were in the sixth or seventh grade. Cindy finally went to visit Mom at the nursing home and assured her that as soon as they could, they would take her back.

I was so grateful to Cindy when she sent an ambulance to pick her up from the old folks' home and took her back to what I called the Looney Bin. Mother was happier there now and I kept trying to assure her that it was temporary until I could figure out something better. Truly though, I was happy that she was there. I felt like she was getting taken care of and was safe. I gave her a cell phone and programmed in several numbers so she could call anyone she wanted.

Her stomach never did improve much. She hardly ate. She would go down to play bingo off and on when she first got there, and she made an attempt to eat in the cafeteria. I visited her often there also. The only time she got out was when I loaded her up and took her outside or for a ride. There was a long covered porch with several chairs in a line by the front door. We sat out there many times. I sometimes would bring her soup or whatever she thought she might eat, but still didn't eat much.

When she needed extra care, Hospice was brought in. They brought her a special mattress because she was hardly getting out of bed and she quit playing bingo or going to eat at the cafeteria.

I don't think anyone else went to visit her much. I know Eldon did a few times. My brother Mark and family visited once near Christmas time -- her last Christmas. Fred was gone to northeast Oklahoma living at the lake with his new girlfriend, Beth and her son. My nephew came from Minnesota once to see her at my urgent request. She never got to see her great nephew though, only pictures. A shame really because my nephew, Isaac, was her favorite and his son looked just like him. My sister, Teresa, was in rehab trying to get herself well, and believe it or not Morris had gone with me once to visit her.

I had talked with a doctor that checked on the residents about Mother's stomach problem. He told me that folks who get C-diff usually don't live much longer than six months. Of course I didn't believe that Mother would ever pass away. She was too mean, too stubborn. But the day did come. In fact, I had read the little books that Hospice had given me to explain what was going on with Mother -- what to expect and how to deal with her passing. I highly recommend both, having Hospice for a person who will be exiting this world and reading the little books and pamphlets.

Mother never was a big eater. She ate like a bird all the years that I knew her. I remember she had called me a few times at night when she needed something and I would call the nurses' station. They were more than happy to go and see what she needed, whether it be a pain pill, a pop, or help with going to the bathroom. She told me that the aides would even sneak into the kitchen to get her some milk or a sprite.

Mother got to where she couldn't even eat the food that they brought to her. I called a friend of my sister's, Ellen, to see if she could go to the rehab center and take Teresa to see Mom. I called my brother Mark and told him he needed to go see Mother and to call Fred. Teresa got there on that last good day. That day when they have energy, you think they are all well and will go on living forever. That day was two days before she passed away. My sister and Ellen took her a McDonald's hamburger, the one with just ketchup and pickles on it and a chocolate shake, both one of her favorite junk food items to nibble on, and I mean nibble. She apparently sat up somewhat, ate and talked plenty. It was a very good visit according to my sister and her friend. I was at work as it was a Friday.

Saturday morning I had the urge to clean out a few kitchen cupboards before going to see Mother. My friend, Sheila, had made some soup and gave me some to take to Mother that day also. Even though I wanted to clean those cupboards before going to see her, something was telling me to hurry. I hurried through only two cupboards and drove to the nursing home. It was about a 30 minute drive from my place.

When I walked into her room, a couple of the Hospice women were with her. I was surprised to see them and asked what was going on, not really wanting to hear the answer. I looked at Mother, she seemed fine. The woman said they were just checking on her and she left the room. I offered the soup to Mom and she acted like she would like to eat some. After a few minutes I got a call on my cell phone. It was the Hospice nurse asking to meet me out by the nurses' station.

Mother was curious when I came back to her room. I told her it was just something I needed to check on. I don't think she really wanted to know. I felt she had her suspicions that I had talked with Hospice, but was not insistent on pursuing any explanation and I was happy about that. "Something has changed," I think she said to me. "Her vitals have changed. She doesn't have much longer." I could hear her words but didn't understand. "She seems fine to me," I said. "Her organs are shutting down. She could pass within a few hours or perhaps more." I wanted to escape. I didn't want to be there when she passed. Perhaps if I left for just a little bit she could go without me seeing it. I didn't think I could bear watching her go as I did with my brother Don.

"I need to go run some errands and then I'll be back." I actually said to the Hospice nurse and she nodded. I had hoped she didn't suspect I was a coward, a bad daughter or something worse. Almost immediately I thought, "You're not going anywhere. How could you leave and let her die alone, all alone. You've been with her through everything; you have to be here for this also, it's your job. Don't let her die alone."

I called my brother Mark. He and his family came a couple hours after I had called him. I think he may have called Eldon because he came by also. I told Mark to get a hold of Fred, but Fred never got there. Mark spent some time alone with mom. I waited out in the hall. I had texted or called Morris to let him know what was happening. He was, after all, supposed to be my boyfriend and I needed some comfort. He did text me off and on throughout the night to see how Mother was doing.

I had noticed about a week or two before this day that when I visited Mom at night and when we watched a TV show, she wasn't really looking at the TV. I would catch her looking at me instead. One of her favorite shows was Law and Order Special Victims Unit. She liked Ice-T and she said the actor Christopher Meloni made her think of my dad -- his mannerism or something. But she was no longer interested in the show or anything for that matter. She was, as explained in the little Hospice book, between this world and the next.

How interesting is that? The spiritual part of her getting ready to depart. Leaving all things earthly behind and not really regretting it or so it seemed. God is merciful.

I sat talking to Mother not knowing how many hours she had left. She did eat a little of Sheila's soup and I put the rest in the refrigerator. I sat close to her bed. She seemed to doze off and on, but only for a few minutes at a time. She would open her eyes and see me still there, by her side as always. Her support, her strength and her partner in what little good there was in our life, and partner in crime as well throughout the years. There I sat by her side as I should. I never left for a while. There was no way that I would have left her to pass alone.

About four o'clock in the evening, she wanted to see her friend Terry. I went out into the hallway and told the nurses. They hurriedly scurried off to find him. Soon he was walking into the room. I moved over to the other side of the room, pulled the curtain and sat on the other bed so they could have some kind of privacy. They had moved her roommate out a couple of nights before. Had her staying in another room so as not to be there when it happened. I never thought of that, but a nice thing to do for not only the roomie but also for the family waiting with their loved one.

Terry sat in the chair but not as close as I had been sitting. They made small talk. I picked up a bible that was on the other bed. The beige curtain that separated the room in half was closed just enough that I couldn't see Mother's upper torso and she couldn't see me. She may have even thought I had left the room. I heard them talk about so and so and how they didn't eat enough, and so and so ate too much and could stand to lose a little weight. There were a few moments of silence, but then a bit more small talk. I smiled. Then there came a long silence. "Jesus loves you, Grace." I started to tear up as I do now. This was a Holy Spirit moment where this somewhat mentally challenged man's mouth uttered these most sacred and meaningful words to a woman who lived thinking she was a sinner and her miserable life was the punishment for her sins -- never believing she could ever be forgiven for her many, many sins. I silently thanked God and hoped she took it to heart.

Terry left the room. A few of the younger staff members came in and loved on her tiny little 63 pound body, actually trying to get into the bed with her. She loved it. They knew she might not be there in the morning or the following day when they came back to work. The hours ticked by. I picked up a small, little spiral notebook and a pen that was sitting on her table and asked her if there was anything she wanted to say to anyone. She shook her head no. I knew she might have had she not been between both worlds now, the other one taking over. The old world drifting away as the stronger pull of the new world taking her away, taking her away from me. I jotted down things she had said to the kids and grandkids in the past. She, after all, had nothing to give them, nothing to leave them. All had been taken, all had been lost.

I asked her if she wanted to pray. She shook her head no. I felt like I should pray out loud for her, but I felt it would be weird reciting them as a child reciting words to a play. She might criticize me as she did when she heard me sing as a child and said I couldn't sing and couldn't carry a tune. I hesitated, but knew I should recite the prayers for her. I thought, 'you have to do this for her. She can't criticize you, she's dying. You can do it; she can never bring it up to you ever, she is dying. She won't remember if you do it too fast or sound stupid, she's dying and she can't come back and criticize you. Say the damn prayers.'

I said I would pray and I began. I recited the Lord's Prayer, the Hail Mary, the one including the Holy Ghost and the

Act of Contrition. I kind of hurried through them and in the end I said, "Oh, I remembered them." As if I could forget the prayers that I prayed so often.

Night was setting in. She wanted some of that 'good soup' Sheila had made. I retrieved it, heated it up and fed her. A few spoonfuls was all she managed. I didn't think 'this is the last thing I will ever do for her.' I don't think I was thinking anything except that I was doing what I was supposed to do. This was my job. God gave her to me to help her through her miserable adult life because she needed help. I was the daughter, but put in a mother's role.

Nurses came in to check her off and on and had given her a shot to ease the pain that comes with organs shutting down. As the night hours continued to tick away, I sat with her. The lights were dulled and as she went to sleep I knew the time was close. I made myself somewhat comfortable in her roomie's recliner, but couldn't sleep. She started to breathe loudly, as like a snore. By morning the breathing, having endured it all night, had almost made me mad. Not angry mad, crazy mad.

When the nurses did come in during the night off and on to check her vitals and turn her, I made sure Mother knew I was there still overseeing her care. Still making sure she was comfortable. Even though she had slipped into a coma like state, I asked if she was in pain and if so, could they please give her more medicine. They assured me they were making sure she was not in pain, etc., and had given her all they could and would check with the doctor.

There was one time that several nurses or aides had come in to turn her. My mother must have heard this one aide that she didn't like. In true Grace like fashion, actually as if in a fit of anger, she kind of lunged toward her and let out a growl like sound. The nurses asked her to leave and they turned to me and told me Mom didn't care for her much and apologized to me for bringing her in to help. Wow, Mother's last angry act. She still had that in her? How appropriate for me to see her last act of defiant anger and meanness.

Six o'clock a.m. -- one of mother's favorite nurses, Mary,

came in. She didn't see me sitting in the chair close by. She was leaving for the day, her shift was over. I saw her look at Mother's fingernails, stroke her hair and then she bent down and kissed her with a loud smack on her forehead. I was so moved, I cleared my throat so that she would know that I was there and that mother was not alone.

The early hours of the morning drifted away, me still by her side. Hospice had come in and checked on both of us. They asked if I needed anything. I did ask them if they could bring me back some Benadryl for the anxiety attack that was sure to come soon. I was surprised it hadn't happened already, but was grateful it hadn't. I did expect to have an attack, especially when she actually passed away. They left. A few hours later the Hospice nurse came back in a rush. The staff had called her back. They knew it was time. She did not bring the Benadryl. We sat by Mother and the nurse talked with me as she watched Mother. Her breathing had changed sometime earlier. It was hesitant and deep and spaced. The nurse said to me, "Okay, say the last thing you want to say to your mama." She got up to leave the room. "I'll be back in a few minutes." I knew it meant Mother was going now. I bent down to hold her as best I could and whispered, "I'll take care of everything." Not "I love you" or "I forgive you and love you!" But "I'll take care of everything." As well as she would have expected me to do as I always had. I felt her last breath on my ear.

The nurse came back in, "Has she stopped breathing?" I said, "Yes, for a little bit again." I guess at that moment I didn't believe she was gone. Gone. It was over, done. Finito. "She's gone," she confirmed. I stood aside. She and another hospice nurse stood beside me rubbing my arm and looking at me. She didn't know I didn't like to be touched, but I allowed it. Shock? Was I in some kind of shock? Where was my anxiety attack? Where was the fast heartbeat, the shortness of breath, the tremors? None. The nurse that was looking up at me because she was really short had paused at rubbing my arm and said, "Maybe your anxiety is all gone now." Wow, that would have been great if by my mother's passing, my almost debilitating at times anxiety was actually gone.

They left the room. I sat in a chair further away from Mother now. I could have sworn I saw her breathing still. They told me that was normal. I didn't want to leave her. Some of the residents and aides wanted to see Grace, so hospice came in to change her and make her look peaceful I guess. I left the room as they prepared her and called my brother, Mark and Morris and I don't know who else, if anyone at that time...I can't remember.

I went back into the room. She did look at peace. They had her holding the rosary beads I had given her years ago, and her right arm cuddling the little stuffed teddy bear my sister had gotten her to prop up her left arm to alleviate the pain from the stroke. She no longer needed it to help with the pain in her left arm. All pain was gone. They did, however, find the teddy bear useful in keeping her jaw closed they told me. The blanket was on her as if she were just asleep. During the next hour, some of the residence came in. Mark came. They left. I waited for the ambulance to come and get her. They told me they would pack up all her things and I could get them at a later date.

After the visiting was done, I found it quite strange that all of a sudden I wanted her to be taken and I leave immediately. I don't know if I felt I had things to do or I was finally free and now it was time for my life to begin, so I hoped. I stood out by the nurses' station as they wheeled her out, but I didn't really look hard to watch as the stretcher carried her down the opposite hall and out into the ambulance. I did feel though, as if I wanted to get into my car and follow them. I started to, but they were at another end of the building and it didn't quite work out that way. I let her go. I let her go without me. She had never, ever really been without me.

"My. Did you feel a sense of relief?"

I've read where psychologists tell us that guilt is one of the strongest emotions that we experience after a loved one has passed on. Guilt for not having done more with or for that person, for not expressing our true feelings or extent of love or perhaps being neglectful at times. I felt no guilt at the time of my mother's death. I have felt sad at times since her passing just thinking about things we could have done together if she would have gone along. I feel like she got cheated out of many years of good life as did I.

I know in my heart that Mother lost a part of herself when my father died. Buss and the drinking had changed her into some kind of person that was unable to be a good mother. Her way of thinking of a happy home and family life must have been stomped out in a moment; her feeling of true love gone forever. She had become a woman desperate to survive in an extremely evil way of life with neither the strength nor knowledge of how to escape. Sad that she never accepted that God would forgive her or had forgiven her.

Relief? I don't think so, not really, but then my job wasn't quite finished. I had to take care of the arrangements and any unfinished or unsettled business. My daughter stepped up and took me to Oklahoma City where they had mother's body for cremation. I picked out a beautiful shiny bronze square urn with one decoration that made me think of the star that the magi followed the night of Christ's birth. I had gone to the Catholic Church that I was a member of years ago when my daughter was growing up. I hadn't really attended regularly since but I had joined a women's group within the church. The pastor had assured me months before, that even though I was not currently a member and Mother was not a member and had never been, they would hold the service for her anyway.

The funeral home wasn't sure they could have her back in my hands by Thursday, but they did. I felt, even though she was not really in that urn, she was and she needed to be at her service. In the meantime, my daughter took me to a Christian Bookstore where I purchased about 50 sheets what I would call church bulletin paper. It had a beautiful print of a gated garden on it and you could fold it in half. I wrote out her obituary over and over to get it as perfect as I could. I put notifications in Norman and Vinita, OK and in Jamestown, NY.

I had asked mother several times if she wanted to go to the little chapel there and pray. She always declined until one day. I took her -- she didn't get out of her wheelchair. I sat a bit behind her in the pew and I hoped that she had made some peace with God that day since it was probably less than a year before she was gone. I told her then that I would make sure we had her service there and we did. I guess whispering in her ear, "I'll take care of everything," included this last act.

The service was a short mass. Everyone was there that should have been. Fred made it but I didn't talk to him. Our friend Lisa had gotten Teresa from rehab, took her to her home to get ready and brought her to the church. I invited Lisa to sit with the family in the pews, after all she was like family. Morris had come into town the night before. He wanted to sit in the back, not with me. I got mad at him so he sat with me. He knew, but I didn't, that he would never be a part of the family and all the other deceptions he hid from me. My daughter sat on one side, he on the other, and he didn't go up to receive communion. I didn't know why until I found out that he really wasn't baptized into the Catholic Church. He lied about that as well as other things.

Father said I didn't have to pay for the singers nor the food that the women's club cooked and served, but I knew Mother would not want charity. I didn't want charity either. I paid and was more than happy to.

My best friend Vinnie had driven three hours to get to the service, but left right after. I thought Morris would stay with me that night also, but he didn't. He left right after the service and the lunch. I really thought he would stay and comfort me. Nope. Gone. He was no support. My friends, Paula, Mary, and my daughter came back to the apartment with me and stayed for a while.

"Where did you bury your mother?"

Haven't. She and my brother Don are in my possession on a nice shelf with family pictures around them. Monsignor Caligiuri told me, "You need to get them in the ground. Don't have them back in a closet somewhere." I assured him that they were not in a closet, and I figure if Jesus comes back and needs their ashes, He knows where they are.

After Mom's passing, I had spent more time with Morris. I

had started to work less than full time so was able to go to his house and stay three or four days a week. I thought we were planning on me moving in with him and finding some part time work in that area, but soon after Mother's death, he was diagnosed with lung cancer. I continued to go to his house. I took him to treatments and continued to clean and mow the lawn. Here again, I thought I should be the caregiver and take care of him until one day I had doubts.

It was a hot summer day, 2008, just about six months after Mom's death. I was driving on my way to see Morris, three hours away, and talking on the phone with my friend Mary about everything. The more I talked about the whole situation, he with cancer and me taking him to treatments and mowing. I started thinking, 'holy shit, I don't want to live like this do I? I'm getting too old for all this work and then to take care of him too?' I'm sure Mary was feeling my agony and probably was trying to help me through the thought process; I just don't remember her words exactly. By the time I got there, I was ready to turn around and go back home. I didn't even take my bag from the truck. I walked in; he had been dozing on the couch. He could tell something was wrong and we began to discuss it. He stood and started to pace a little and became teary eyed and said, "So you're leaving me?" I truly felt that it hurt him. I had never seen this side of him, but I did know how selfish he was. I felt it was not so much that I was leaving him as it was he wouldn't have such a kind, loving, do all kind of woman around. He had left a little note one day for me that said, "You are the hardest working person I have ever known and I am blessed to have you."

We were supposed to go to dinner at his cousin Dorothy's that evening. Both she and her sister Joyce were going to be there and had invited us over. I had met Joyce briefly once before and I had seen Dorothy and talked to her many times, but these were the only two of his family that I had actually met. I went with him, but we were strained and they could tell there was something wrong. I spent some time alone out on the back porch trying to smell the lake water that was close by. I think he may have told them something while I was out there. I was cordial and enjoyed the dinner. We went back to his house, I stayed around and he tried to be charming as usual. I started to feel as if it was more right to stay with him than not. I decided to spend the night. "So you love me again, huh?" He said. "You stayed around long enough to fall back in love with me." I don't remember my response, but I did get into bed with him that night. I actually felt like leaving in the middle of the night. Funny, because in the morning he actually said, "I thought you were going to get up in the middle of the night and sneak off." "I thought about it," I told him.

By November and after working my ass off at his place and taking him to treatments and driving back and forth and working in Norman, the last straw was when he would not...again...for the third year, spend Thanksgiving with me at Vinnie's house. It was only thirty minutes from his house. That was it, I had had it. I wrote him a letter and sent his house keys back to him. I asked for my keys back and to mail my personal things that were there also. I think he didn't believe it was over, but it was. I am sure we talked on the phone some, but I was moving on. I couldn't get my full time job back because I had given it up and they hired someone else. I had some money so the part time was all right for a while. I thought I would start writing again or getting into more of the music aspect. All I know is that at that time I wanted to start to live for me. I had so many responsibilities since the age of nine, and here I was fifty six years old and not much to show for it, any of it.

Morris had sent back all of my things except for my house key and my slippers. I never did get the key back, and he admitted he liked seeing my slippers by the bed. I finally did get those back, but never the key.

A few months before our breakup, Morris had been at my house because he had to have an eye operation for a detached retina. When he had to go back to Oklahoma City for another appointment for his eye, we were not an item anymore. His sister who had come from Nevada to stay with him for a while took him. They got hotel rooms and he texted me asking if I would come and see him. I did not and had no desire to. I was kind of glad I didn't have to go pick him up, take him to the doctor and then take him home, three hours away and then come home again. Plus I was just plain angry with him. I had wasted another seven years with someone that had no intention of commitment.

"Did you ever see Morris again?"

Of course, but not like you might think. There was a commercial on T.V., "Boy Meets Girl," etc. It was one of those phone numbers you could call and listen to men or women who had placed ads looking for someone. I called and placed an ad describing myself and what I was looking for. By God I was going to get it right or that was it. I would have been fine to be alone though, I was at that point. I left it on there for about three months. I had a piece of paper and made notes as to who I thought I would talk to further or not, based on messages they had left me.

Even as I talked to them on the phone, I continued to cross them off. I did have a date for Valentine's Day. He was nice enough, but we both knew we weren't for each other. I talked to some men that seemed to have lots of money and property and homes, but they seemed to be drinkers and smokers. "Why, you'd be just the woman to get me to stop." Yeah, right. I was not looking for a project or any problems. No stress or heartache either. I met a nice Native American, John. I loved talking with him on the phone -- he had a very sexy voice. We met and he was very intelligent. Although I liked him, I wasn't seeing me with him. I just wasn't feeling it. There was about a week left of my ad and I had decided I was going to stop for a while with my quest. There was one man on there that sounded interesting. I liked his voice and he just seemed sweet. I had left him a couple of messages, but no response. Finally I left my phone number on one of my messages because, as I said, I was going to stop my little ad.

I did get a call back from him. His name was Kenneth, but I felt like he lived a bit too far from Norman. He was probably about an hour and a half away from me, and I was tired of the long distance relationships. Anyway, we started talking some but I was still talking to John and a couple of other men. I finally agreed to meet with Kenneth and this one other man on the same day. I know that sounds familiar, like my past, but, hey, I'm a fast operator sometimes. I wanted to see what they looked like. I told the one man that I was going to Academy Sports to get a battery for my boat, so I met him there. All the time this guy and I had talked previously on the phone, he just invited me to his place, not out to eat or anything, just to his house. Of course I never went, but I did want to see what he looked like. So we met, shopped around and talked. He looked -- I swear like Dick Tracy, the comic strip Tracy, not Warren Beatty who played Tracy in a movie. Now that might have made a difference. I knew immediately, though, I didn't care to pursue him. He called later and still invited me to his home.

I told Kenneth I would meet him at some restaurant because he wanted to take me out to eat. I went from Academy to a Walmart parking lot to meet with him. I arrived sooner than he and parked. We were having a hard time figuring out where I was parked. He said he was in a green Taurus when indeed when I saw it, it looked beige to me. Also when I saw him just from the window of his car, I knew I didn't want to go to a restaurant to eat with him. I asked him if he didn't mind pulling into the Sonic close by and he could buy me a coke. That was fine with him.

We pulled in side by side. I got out of my truck and into his car. Oh my God. The car was messy and it was covered in red dust in and out of the car. Red dust from the shale on the roads that he traveled every day and it smelled badly of the dust. He ordered us drinks. I took a quick look and assessment of him, and I knew there was no way I would be with this guy. His hair was cut really short. I think he had somewhat a faint mustache; he was heavy and seemed to be wearing not so clean or perhaps just not ironed clothes. I remember black jean like slacks, an almost white shirt and black cowboy boots.

He was happy to have finally met. He explained again how, "When I heard your voice, I knew I just had to meet you," and why it took him so long to get back with me. The background story is that his wife of 29 years had passed away in January. She had a massive heart attack after her shift at a convenience store, and here we were meeting sometime in late March.

We finished our drinks and I made my escape. I saw him watch me get into my truck. It reminded me of this one time when I went to the movies with this creepy guy who put his arm around me and stared at me about the whole time we were there. It was the movie Pearl Harbor with Ben Affleck -- I love Ben Affleck. I had thought about telling this creepy guy that I had to go to the bathroom and then get in my car and leave, but I really wanted to see this movie and I figured he would probably want to escort me anyway. By the time the movie was over, my back was hurting so badly because I was so tense and in a position of hugging the opposite side of my chair as much as I could through the whole movie and, it is a very long movie.

He walked me to my car and asked me something weird or told me something like how he had a pair of women's boots and would I wear them if we made love. Creepy, creepy, creepy.

Anyway so I drove away from Kenneth and called him later that night. "I know you are not the one, but we can talk on the phone because I know you are lonely and I am lonely," I said to him. I didn't want to hurt him and we had started somewhat of a friendship, but I couldn't see me with him, not one bit. He was okay with that. Actually, he would have taken anything I should happen to dole out.

I was talking to Kenneth and to John, the Indian, working and enjoying my life. Then guess who needed me.

"Morris. And you helped him."

I think he had a doctor's appointment in Oklahoma City and asked if he could stay with me that night before heading home the next day. By now I was through being angry with him and told him he could. I knew I was not going to sleep with him and had no desire to. He came to my house, still had the key and let himself in. I was at work. We ate at the house but he didn't seem to feel too well. He made a call to his aunt in Missouri and was a bit emotional. When it came time to sleep, he decided he would be fine on the couch. I went to bed. In the morning, he was worse.

He was having difficulty breathing. I told him, "You've got to go to a hospital. I can take you to some local hospital where they'll probably kill you." You hear things, you know. "I can take you to the VA hospital in Oklahoma City." After all it was the VA that had been treating him for his cancer. "Or you can go home." He said I could take him to the VA. He could only take a step or two at a time before attempting to walk again. Morris was a big man, tall and heavy. There is no way I could have even braced him if I wanted to. I drove his truck up as close as I could to the door. I helped him get dressed and his shoes on. He finally got to the bathroom and then out to the truck. I guided him, but that's all I could have done should he have started to fall.

His oxygen level was 10! It should have been 100. "Thank God you got him here in time!" the doctors said at the VA. hospital. So began yet another juggling act. He was admitted to the hospital, of course. I was back and forth, working and talking to Kenneth every night, sometimes for hours at a time -- well into the midnight hour. I'd leave work, drive to Oklahoma City, sit and visit and help Morris with showers and going to the bathroom and fetching help or pop or ice cream down the hall. I was at the point where I couldn't wait to leave there though and call Kenneth on my way home.

"Oh?"

Yes, I enjoyed talking to Kenneth. Here was a man who actually cared enough to listen to me. He was actively involved in our conversations, it was not all about him. When we began to talk about our children, I realized that he was a different sort of man than I was accustomed to. He was an actual family man. He talked a lot about his deceased wife. I could understand that and I felt sad for him. I probably told him as little as I could about my marriages and Morris, but no more than that. I didn't want to scare him off. He was a country boy born and raised country; what would he know of such a woman as I had been.

We watched TV together on the phone. He waited on the phone when I had to go to the bathroom or change into my jammies, or I would call him back after my shower. Morris would have never done any of those things. Never. It was all one sided with him. All about him. Well, as you know, all of my men were pretty much the same. I had come to call them, "selfish, self-centered, sap sucking, sons of bitches!"

The doctors came into Morris's room a few days after his admittance, tests and MRI's complete, and told him he had about three months to live. Neither of us seemed to react in any way much. I was secretly trying to figure out the main doctor's accent. I knew it was Middle Eastern, but couldn't quite place it. "Do either of you have any questions?" he asked. Morris had none; I was a bit obsessed with wanting to know where he was from and asked. "Lebanon?" I know, a bit cold asking that question. I mean what else could you ask when they tell you or someone they have three months to live. "Are you sure? Really?" Or do you want to go into asking, "What is the process? What can I expect to happen?" I think not. I know the group probably thought, "What is her deal asking such a question?" I didn't care. I would never see them again; and, I really wanted to know where he was from because I couldn't quite get it from his accent or his color. I knew a Lebanese guy once but for such a short time that I can hardly remember anything about him.

Morris asked me to call his daughter and tell her. I delivered the news as gently as I could, but how can you give that kind of news gently? I figured by saying it slowly was gently. Now mind you, I had only spoken to her once before when she thanked me for taking care of her daddy when I was taking him to his cancer treatments. My only words to her then were, "It's alright." This day I had to tell this stranger that the doctors gave her daddy three months to live. She burst into crying and asked me or yelled is more like it, "How could they tell someone that? That they only have three months to live?" I assured her that her dad wanted to know and they told him. She decided she was coming to Oklahoma. She lived in California. He asked me to call his cousin, Dorothy, and his ex-wife Nicola.

A few days later his son, Kenny, had come to see him. I liked Kenny. I had met him when I visited Morris in California a few times. He reminded me of James Dean. He wanted me to listen to some of his rapping one time. I thought he was pretty good. He told his dad once that he felt sorry for me when he came home one day and found me scrubbing the kitchen floor on my hands and knees. Well, it needed it badly and that is the best way to get a floor really clean I think.

When I had gone to California, Morris either wanted Kenny to move out or was trying to teach him to be more responsible and wouldn't buy groceries or toilet tissue. I didn't mind the food being low, but I needed more toilet tissue if I was going to be there for a few days. One time I gave Kenny some money and asked him to go to the store and get toilet tissue and whatever he wanted. When he returned I handed him a few rolls of tissue for his own bathroom and he thanked me. He was out of high school and was into surfing, as his father was I guess when he was younger, although Morris told me he was still surfing when I met him at fifty-nine. I found out that he told lots of lies and stories so I doubt he was surfing at fifty-nine. I hope he was, but doubt it.

Kenny came to Oklahoma to see his dad and went back to Vegas. Morris's daughter, Christina, arrived. I met her at the airport. I had only seen a picture of this beautiful woman and her beautiful mother once. The picture was large and on the fireplace at Morris's. I asked him, "Who are these models and why do you have such a large picture of them?" He told me it was his daughter and her mother. I couldn't believe it. They looked about the same age and so beautiful. Her mother's singing group sang a song titled, "Angel Baby," and I heard Christina quietly sing it to her dad while he was in the hospital.

I pulled into the airport pick up lane to wait for Christina. I wasn't sure I would recognize her. Finally, out walks this beauty, but she was brunette, not blonde like the picture. Regardless, it was her. I almost got lost driving back to the VA. Hospital because I was not that familiar with the Westside of Oklahoma City. We finally made it back and she stayed in the hospital with her dad twenty-four seven until his release. I still went there after work, but always went home at night. I did stay all night one time before she arrived, but didn't feel it necessary for me to do so again. Christina slept on the hard floor the whole time she was there. She and I texted while in the room about issues at hand and concerns she had without bothering or worrying her dad.

One day a nurse came in and said to Morris, "Your wife called and asked if you would call her back," or something like that. All I focused on was, "Your wife called." I asked him "Why would she say your wife?" "Oh, it's Niky," he replied. I still didn't understand why Nicola referred to herself as his wife -- maybe just to get information about him or attention. I didn't know until Morris told me a few days later that they weren't really divorced. I about lost it. All these years I thought they were divorced. "Well, we were legally separated." Which I found out later wasn't true either. They never bothered to do the paperwork. Seven years I was in a relationship with him! Seven years!

It really didn't matter now anyway. It was just another bad choice I had made. Morris began calling me his "guardian angel" from then on, and how I saved his life. He believed he made it to my house so I would get him to the hospital to give him whatever time he had left to see his kids again. His son, Joe, had come to Oklahoma also to see his dad, then Christina's husband and their darling little girls. His sister, niece and cousins also came to see him. Even a friend of his, a woman who I suspected he had tried to hit on because I actually heard some of their conversation through the phone one night when it accidentally called my number, came to see him.

His daughter had met a lawyer on the plane coming into Oklahoma, called him and he came to the hospital to draw up power of attorney papers. I know there was some kind of draft written up about a will, but don't know if was ever made legal. Lots of things were happening and I was still there because Morris wanted me there. I would go out into the waiting area because I didn't need to be there while family was visiting, and he would send someone out to get me. He wanted me with him. I was still acting as the girlfriend in his eyes I guess. I was helping with the showers and to the bathroom, etc., still. I was making sure he was comfortable and asking the nurses to do this or that -- whatever was needed, and I was asking questions as to why they were doing something or did he need those stockings on, etc.

"What about Kenneth?"

Oh, that was still going on. In fact, one night he was going to be in Norman with his son. They were going to a dance at the Moose Lodge that I was a member of. They were getting in as guests of the band. I was going to meet him there, but Morris was not feeling very well and I hated to leave him too soon so I stayed. It became too late to drive home, get ready and meet Kenneth at a reasonable hour.

Kenneth and I continued to talk on the phone. I don't remember how many weeks Morris was in the hospital, but then came the time when they dismissed him. I saw him two more times when he had to go back to the VA. for checkups, and the last time I asked him about Nikola. He said he thought he had told me they weren't divorced. "Why wouldn't I tell you?" I sternly replied a bit loudly, "Because you knew I would have never been with you had I known that you weren't divorced!" We had tea and I kissed him goodbye.

His daughter drove him back to his home in eastern Oklahoma. Soon they had a sale of his things and packed the rest of the stuff up and had it driven in a trailer back to California. She and her dad with his oxygen tank flew back to California, and he lived with her for a while. When he landed he called me, "I will send for you, I promise." He swore he was bringing me out there.

So Morris was in California, basically out of my life even though we texted or talked once in a while. I remember he told me something that was bothering him, and I called his daughter and talked to her about it. It was something to do with his meds for which I had known about and helped him with, and also about how he was feeling physically. Well, that didn't go over very well with Christiana. So it ended me trying to help him with anything further. He was in her care now and they could deal with it.

Once Morris left the VA. hospital, I began going out with Kenneth. We had managed to meet at the Moose Lodge a few times and went out to dinner. We were sort of dating, but I wasn't counting on much. I had previously tried to pawn him off on a couple of girlfriends. I thought he was just too nice for me.

I don't remember the order in which the following took place, but I had Kenneth over one evening for pizza and a movie. He showed up with those same black slacks and he looked dumpy in them. I didn't sit on the couch with him. I sat in my recliner. Another time I agreed to meet Kenneth at the Moose Lodge. I had previously mentioned liking longer hair and goatees and soon these things started to appear on him. He was also wearing his cowboy hat and better jeans. What I didn't know was that he was a pretty big guy but had lost a lot of weight after his wife had passed away. That is why his clothes didn't fit well.

We met again at the Moose. We started, or I should say I started, to enjoy being with him. He paid attention to me. He bought me drinks, we danced and had a good time. I invited him to follow me home one night after the dance and he started to massage my shoulders. I didn't know he would try to massage a bit further down my front as he did, but he did. I guess he asked if it was okay and because I was a little drunk, I turned around from my seated position on the floor, got on my knees and showed him my breasts. 'Boobies,' as I called them later when we laughed about it. I knew he hadn't seen any as beautiful as mine. Hell, the guy had only been with two women and he married both of them. This was probably the night that before I did this, we had been kissing outside at the Moose on a picnic table. He was a great kisser and he said to me while looking into my eyes, "You would be so easy to fall in love with." Wow, what a smooth talker. And so began our love story.

CHAPTER TWENTY-TWO

I was sitting at my desk at work one day when a delivery man came in with some flowers. I was sure they were for my friend, Jill, who had recently started dating this guy from her church. I was so surprised when he said my name with a question mark at the end. My pleasantly surprised response was, "That's me!" I knew they had to be from Kenneth. The card read, "To someone special." Not only had I never ever gotten flowers delivered to me at work, but I was so impressed that he had spelled my name right, and he had to have listened to where I had worked, and had to have looked up the address. Now I was starting to like this guy.

I didn't mention the flowers right away when he called that night. He told me later that he was really getting upset because he thought that would be the first thing I would mention if they had actually gotten delivered that day as the florist promised. But by me not saying anything, he thought they hadn't gotten to me. Finally, he asked and I acted like I didn't want to say anything because I didn't really know they were from him. I was teasing of course, but I didn't want him to think he was the only guy pursuing me.

I changed his name to Kord because I was managing two men that were named Ken or Kenneth. I told him I couldn't call him that without thinking of them, so I asked what his middle name was. That wasn't going to work either because my sister had dated a creep with that name. So I came up with Kord and he liked it.

I joked with him one evening. We were sitting on the couch and he said, "You're so beautiful." I told him, "I can't believe you think that." "I don't think it, I know it," he said. "I know what happened," I said as I put my hand on his forehead,

"From now on, your name shall be Kord and you will see nothing but beauty when you look at her." I laughed and said, "That must be what God said to you." He just smiled at me as he did when he was amused by my silly actions or thoughts. So all of my friends and family met him, liked him immediately and became acquainted with Kord -- soon to become my Kordiepoo.

I didn't know there were men like this, so loving, so attentive and just wanting to make me happy. He would always tell me I was beautiful and actually listened to the things I was willing to share with him. I was myself with him. Completely and wholly myself and he liked me. Kord came to see me once a week until he had to see me more often, and would come down in the middle of the week. We would lie in bed at night, he holding me and we'd talk for hours. I loved when he would tell me story after story of his childhood, growing up in the country and all of his mischief.. We spent many nights laughing. I loved his stories. I loved that he had a wonderful childhood and grew into this wonderful man: sensitive, loving, considerate, caring and unselfish. I didn't deserve to be with such a man. I didn't know how to accept someone actually thinking I was beautiful and also truly falling in love with me.

Little by little Kord was becoming my best friend, and I let him see exactly who I was and what I was like as I did with my girlfriends. I never really had a man for a friend because they always wanted to sleep with me. Well, I had one that was a friend, but he was actually in love with me I believe, and he was married, so we were friends. But other than that, perhaps Jerry, my accountant friend, because he had no interest in me that way. I was myself with Kord as I had never been with any of my other serious relationships. I don't know why that was except maybe I thought they wouldn't like me or love the real me. Many women do this and I wish that we wouldn't. I felt like I was in a cage, especially with David and Morris. Why did I think they were so great and that I didn't measure up? How do men do that to women? Where do they learn the technique of manipulating women like that? Oh hell, where did my mother learn manipulation? I must say, I was used to manipulation, although

Mother also included the art of making me feel guilty or perhaps that came from being Catholic.

So Kord was in love with me. I was trying to accept his love. I told him I decided to only see him and see where this was going to lead. He was very happy. We became closer, although I was still not trusting much of anything, was holding back, guarding my being. After all this was my last try at finding the right man. I had pledged that I was going to not accept anything less than exactly what I wanted in a man or I was finished looking. I was 56 and fine with being alone. After all, I had always taken care of myself pretty much and they had always caused me heartache and setbacks. I had walked away with nothing in all of my serious relationships.

My friend, Connie, came from Cape Cod to visit and attend our all school, high school reunion. We shared a hotel room and after a few drinks with friends invited a couple of girlfriends to the room, Carol and Candy. I always had a special love in my heart for Carol. Not sure why but she was always this quiet kind of shy little girl and I just liked her. Her family actually took my brother, Don, in to live with them during his high school years, and he considered her older brother to be his best friend.

Even though I was visiting with my girlfriends, it seemed like I was on the phone a lot also with both Morris and Kord. Morris had called, feeling left out I guess, and just wanting my attention even though there was nothing left there on my part. Kord had called. He actually had been in a bit of an accident but was all right, and he was my boyfriend and had the right to call me.

I was also in between vehicles and was driving a van that David gave me to try out. Thank God Connie and I actually made it to Vinita and back because a few days later, a motor mount broke.

"David your ex?"

Yes, he was still providing me with vehicles. He took that one back and gave me another.

"Do you think he continued to do this out of guilt or did he

still care for you?"

Maybe a little of both. Many of my men had only good things to say about me or continued to have a soft spot in their heart for me. Some even wanted me back, such as Morris and Brent and M.C., so possibly David would have too.

Kord was late to arrive at my house for dinner one night about six months after we had started dating. I didn't really question why. I guess, I thought he had run into bad traffic or something. We ate dinner and were relaxing on the couch watching a movie. At some point I noticed a bag behind the couch pillow, and thought my sister had left something of hers there earlier in the day. I reached for it and saw it was a bag from Helzbergs. I was very surprised. Kord was smiling and said he wondered when I was going to see it. "That's why I was late, and I hid it there when you went into the other room."

It has always been very hard for me to accept gifts. Not that I ever received that many, but still I didn't know how to accept them. I don't know what that stems from, perhaps not feeling worthy of anything; not worthy of being treated nice or getting nice gifts. I assumed it was earrings. I reached in. It could have been a ring box, but I still assumed earrings. I opened the box and there was an exact ring that I would have picked out for myself had I wanted. First I was shocked, secondly, how did he know the exact cut, a marquee cut diamond on gold, not silver, gold as I would have picked. He said, "I know people probably don't do it anymore, but it's like a promise ring." He was so adorable and the moment was so adorable, it made me feel like a teenager -- well what I assume a teenage girl would feel like had she gotten a promise ring. He asked if I liked it and would I wear it. "I love it and it fits perfectly, and how did you know what I would like and my size and of course I'll wear it!"

Kord had farmed and raised livestock just about all of his life, but he was also a self-taught auctioneer. One night when he was auctioning some livestock at a local stockyard, he took a moment to call me in between sets. He ended with, "I love you, babe." He said it got real quiet. He looked up to find everyone looking at him. "Does she love you back?" There was laughter. "What's for dinner?" Another yelled. And still another, "Are we gonna have to start payin' admission to get in here?" He said there was so much laughter and then he realized he had left the mic on while talking to me.

Soon after, Kord began to say he loved me. I hadn't said it. One time I accidently said, "I love you" after he had said it and dropped me off at the front door of a casino. I didn't mean to, it was just a natural response. My sister and friend, Sheila, were with us. I told my sister what I accidently did and she said, "You need to tell him you love him." I said "No, I'm not ready." He joined us and had a big smile on his face. He mentioned what he thought I had said and I denied it, trying not to smile, and left it at that. Soon after that one day we were out by the lake and I asked Kord to pull over. We walked down onto a dock. There is where I told him, "I love you."

Six months after I accepted the promise ring, Kord paced for a few minutes as I sat waiting to go to dinner. In old fashioned style, he got down on one knee ever so close to me and with glassy eyes asked if I would marry him. I said, "Yes!" with the most sincere, heartfelt emotion. I could tell by his glassy eyes and change of breathing that I had just made him very happy as he slipped the ring on my finger.

I didn't want to leave Norman, and I didn't want to live in his country home. It only made sense though to move closer to where he worked and had land. He bought another home for us closer to Oklahoma City, and we were married by an Episcopalian priest in our backyard with family and friends as witnesses. This was the marriage that was real, and I didn't have to sneak and keep it a secret as I did with Ron and David. I wanted a real wedding this time, and I had it, string quartet and everything. I was extremely happy that day. The next morning, we took off for our honeymoon. We drove east and south toward Texas visiting casinos and lakes on the way. I didn't want to go very far. Actually I was unable to go very far without having an anxiety attack, so we opted to stay within the state and just go on an adventure. The second night and very close to Texas, I had an attack. I was lying in bed and started to freak out. Wait a minute, I thought. I am way the hell away from home and with this guy I hardly know and I got married! So began my panic attack.

Now it's not as if I hadn't been having them because I had. After all I had gone through many changes after my mother passed away. I also had many attacks just trying to deal with a new life with Kord. I had been prescribed valium to take, but hated to take them. The doctor told me that I could take Benadryl and that should calm me down. It worked also, but it also makes me sleepy and groggy for a long time. Just one and I just want to sleep, but the valium was worse. I could be a zombie for two days on that stuff and not even a whole pill. I was out of Benadryl so I told Kord that if I didn't have one I was going to have to take a valium or rather half of a valium because that's what I took and it still made me a zombie. I really wanted him to get me some Benadryl, but he didn't understand what I was saying, I guess, so I took the other and for the rest of the trip home I was this zombie walking around just wanting to sleep.

CHAPTER TWENTY-THREE

One day about a year and a half after mom's death, Eldon had gone over to my brother Mark's who lives in the country. He asked my nephew and his friend if they wanted to target shoot. The boys set up some cans, and as they turned toward Eldon, they saw that he had propped the rifle on a tree stump and shot himself in the head. What a terrible thing for them to see.

Fred was staying there at the time, and they said the police had to pull him off of Eldon when they got there. He was crying over him. Eldon, as weird as he was and not a good influence because of the drugs, was like a father to my brothers and sister. So they were all upset. I personally didn't care. I was angry, though, for him doing such a thing in front of those teenage boys. The evidence that showed he intended to kill himself that day was due to the fact that he made sure his dog had plenty of water, and he had cut open and left on the kitchen floor a large bag of dog food in case no one went to his house for a few days.

"Oh my, God. It just doesn't end does it? Where was his girlfriend?"

My understanding was that she would get mad at him off and on and go home to Missouri to her mother's. She happened to be gone that weekend to Missouri. A few weeks after Eldon's suicide, his house caught on fire, something electrical, and the dog died.

"God. And the girlfriend?"

I guess she wasn't there at the time. Later I heard she move to Missouri for good.

Fred had been living with Mark for a year after Mother died, and he got Mark to start drinking again. Well, maybe it wasn't his entire fault. Mark may have started drinking again after twelve years of sobriety due to mother's death, and then Eldon killing himself probably didn't help matters. Regardless, Fred was a bad influence on Mark because Fred kept drinking, and so therefore, Mark did as well. It didn't take long until there was conflict and fighting at that house. When I got either phone calls or texts about the turmoil out there, I kept telling Mark that Fred had to go. He had to find somewhere else to live. There were places he could go, get a job and start some kind of life.

Fred may have not had much of a chance in life. He didn't work much in his 45 years of life. He had two daughters with a woman that he never married. I believe they loved each other, but she couldn't deal with his drinking and not working. He had gone to prison a couple of times, once for a non-contested sex offender charge. They, mother and Fred, say it was more a woman scorned. She wanted Fred and he didn't want to be with her, so she said he touched her son. The other time was for not reporting to the sheriff's office when he moved to a different county. I don't know if he did anything to the child, but I figured he was really paying for not only his sin for touching my daughter, but also paying for his dad's sin for touching me.

He had started staying with one of his good friends not too far from Mark's. I would say it was the summer of 2012 when I got a call from Fred's friend telling me, "Freddie came in from the store last night. He got my kids some ice cream, but they were already in bed. I was watching a movie and Fred said he was going outside to look at the stars. I went to bed. I guess he never came in all night. I went out in the yard and found him in the lawn chair looking up at the sky, but he was gone."

I had to tell Mark and Teresa, of course. The medical examiner said he had alcohol, Xanax and methadone in his system.

"Did he commit suicide?"

I am not sure. He may have made a mistake and accidentally had too many bad things in his system, trying to cope with the pain -- the pain that alcoholics and drug addicts talk about, the pain they can't deal with. I don't understand what they are talking about. I had pain and lots of pain throughout the years. I didn't drown the pain. I didn't stifle it with drugs. I dealt with it and continued on. I dealt with the life that was thrust upon me, and I dealt with the life I made because of my mistakes.

"You sound angry about his death."

I'm angry with the waste of his life. I'm angry with the waste of Mother's life and the weakness of my family.

"You love them regardless."

Yes. When I talked to Monsignor Caligiuri about Fred, he told me not to judge him. It took me a very long time to stop judging him and not liking him, until finally I felt sad and guilty and have forgiven him as well as everyone else.

CHAPTER TWENTY-FOUR

Morris and I continued to talk off and on until he passed away, but not in three months. He lived four more years and always thanked me, his "guardian angel" for saving his life and giving him more time with his family. I am pretty sure that a lot a prayer and God's grace gave him this allotted time.

I got the call. Morris's ex-wife, but not his ex-wife, Nikola. I knew instantly that he was gone. She asked if this was Georgianne, I said "Yes." She announced who she was and I replied, "Oh no," and she told me he had died. "I thought he was doing so well, what happened?" It was a massive heart attack. I didn't understand until she explained about an enlarged heart due to his lungs not working as well as they should and also a valve problem. I was surprised that she had called to tell me. I had expected his daughter or cousin, Dorothy. Dorothy did call a few days later about his passing. Nikola continued to call or text a few times after, telling me about a lot of drama going on between her, her son and Morris's other children from his first marriage. I found out that Morris was not a navy seal, not a Catholic and had another girlfriend as long as he had me, only she was in California, not to mention that he had never divorced Nikola.

Morris never knew that after our final breakup, Dorothy had told me about this other woman and that he had even brought her to Oklahoma to live with him. She had stayed for four months before returning to California because she didn't like Oklahoma. That is one reason why I wasn't invited to his home when he first moved here.

Nikola put many things into perspective when she said, "I think Morris was afraid to be alone." Knowing him, I would say that was probably correct or like a sailor, one in every port.

I had a conversation with Kord that I was going through

many different emotions, and he was very understanding. I told him that in a way, I was relieved Morris was gone. "He was the one man that I would have been stupid enough to go back to." My husband replied, "Even if you were with me?" I assured him, "No, only if I was alone." My husband said, "Well, I felt bad for you, but I was relieved." The next morning I said, "When I said relieved last night, that might not have been the right word. Perhaps freedom is a better word. I feel a sense of freedom."

Once again, I was in a good position. I was at peace with my new life with Kord. I was feeling creative again and started to write. One day I called Allison, my little singer friend, and she told me she was setting up her own studio in her grandparents' house. I thought that was quite an ambitious thing to do. That way she could produce her own CD's, not have to have it done for her.

I asked if there was anything I could help her with, and I am so glad that she said she needed a laptop for the studio. I told her I could help her with that. I had felt bad all these years for not really doing anything for her when I said I would do anything I could. Finally, I could actually do something for her.

It's not a good feeling when you have a thought or sense of something that you just can't shake. This is the God's honest truth. When I knew that Allison drove to a lot of places, either to work or to sing somewhere, I always worried about her, just as a mother would worry about their child out on the roads. I worried about her when I knew specifically when she was driving. I even made sure if we were on the phone or texting, that she was not driving. You know how young people are.

Allison wanted me to come and see her studio, so I had arranged to go to Norman and do that as well as take care of some business with my sister. While I was there, Allison and I could go get a computer. I had called around Norman but did not find a good deal. I had just bought myself a new laptop by a local business in my town, so I gave him a call. I wanted Allison to be present in order to pick out the computer that contained all she needed to perform the tasks for recording music.

A few days went by and the business I needed to do for my sister did not pan out. As much as I didn't want Allison to drive to our house because I worried about her, I did ask her if she wanted to come up so she could pick out the computer she wanted. I thought I'd die if she had a wreck coming up here. It was about an hour or so drive to our house, oh my, and then she would have to drive home. So needless to say, I worried a lot that day, but we did get her a laptop. I told her, smiling, "I do expect you to do great things with it." I started to say the words "And I expect you to record one of my songs," but quickly took them back saying, "I don't expect you to do anything for me, but maybe someday you will record some of my songs, if you think they are good enough." She agreed and thanked me over and over. Such a good girl.

"So all that worrying for nothing, right?"

Ah, no! One night Kord and I went to an Elks Lodge close to our house where Allison was singing. It was spring, and with spring and the heat from the west and the cool from the coast, you start to get bad thunderstorms, hail, high winds and tornadoes in Oklahoma.

That night storms were expected. We went anyway. I hadn't heard her sing in a very long time and wanted to be there to support her. It hailed badly that night. Allison had just recently bought a new car and she was worried about the hail. Luckily it sounded bigger than it was.

This just happened to be the day after I had heard that Morris had passed away, and I was going through a lot of emotions so I was kind of quiet. I sent a note to her mother, several weeks after that, about how although I love hearing her sing, I worried about her. I didn't express to her that what I did not like was seeing several older men talking to her. I mean they would come in and call her name and shake hands with her and they would all talk. I know that it was probably people who knew her and maybe some of it was business, but it bothered me. Then I had to stop and think when I was twenty-four, twenty-five, I was pretty smart about business and schmoozing; however, she was like a daughter to me. She was in my heart, so I worried.

"Yes, I understand worrying about certain things but did

you have to worry about everything?"

Apparently. About a month after that, I had texted her but didn't hear back from her. I figured she would get back to me soon. I knew she had had a gig at the same lodge a couple of weeks before that and another one coming up at a new club. I was just checking in with her as I had been doing. I was anxious about her new CD she was going to produce. I thought I might send a copy on to Alice, and perhaps she would think it was good enough to send to Reba.

I didn't hear back from her. I saw the day after I knew she had that gig that she had been in a horrific car accident. What's weird also is that I had a little bit of an anxiety attack about 1:40 a.m., which I thought was strange, because I hadn't had one in a long time and there didn't seem to be any reason for me to have one.

One of her cousins had posted pictures of the car on Facebook, and one of my favorite pictures of her where she looks like an angel. I quickly read fearing the worst and found out just how bad it was, but that she was alive. I was able to talk briefly to her father on the phone the next day when I located the hospital she was in. I talked to her grandfather the following day, and he revealed that she had sustained a broken back, a broken arm, wrist, leg and ankle. There was some internal bruising I believe because someone mentioned that on Facebook.

It was pouring that night. Allison just about took a wrong exit and tried to correct. The car flipped several times and landed upside down. At some point she managed to crawl out of the crushed car. She managed to get out of something like a concrete drainage channel area and about another 60 yards where she crossed over a road and made it to an Olive Garden. She then tried to throw a rock into a window but did not have the strength to do so. The accident happened at 2 a.m. She was found at seven a.m. The doctors said it was a miracle she could crawl with all those injuries -- it didn't seem possible to them. "She was facing two to five years of rehabilitation," her grandfather said.

He also told me that they thought she would live, and then

a few days later he said she was out of the woods. I could not imagine what she or the family was going through. I was consumed with heartache for Allison. When I slept I had dreams about her, and when awake I couldn't keep myself busy enough to not think about her.

I emailed Alice about Allison and asked her, because Allison is more of a country singer/songwriter, could she or her family or Reba contact her to encourage her in some way. I didn't want her to be discouraged, nor did I want her to give up on her dreams. That very evening I had texted Allison's grandfather and he texted back how she was doing, and that Reba McEntire had called Allison to check on her. I talked with him the next day and he filled me in about Allison and the accident and about Reba calling. He said that she knew it was Reba on the phone and that Reba told her she could send her samples of her work.

I was so happy to hear this. The McEntire family are 'good people' as they would say. I immediately emailed Alice and thanked her for getting the message to Reba and to please thank Reba for me. I felt I had to encourage Allison to get well, get strong and accomplish her dreams.

You often wonder why you meet someone and there is some kind of connection, or you feel like you need to know that person. Sometimes you end up knowing why, sometimes not. Sometimes it may be to your benefit -- sometimes to theirs.

I am happy to say that Allison has made miraculously huge steps in her recovery, continues to sing, recorded a new CD, and I believe intends on sending it on to Reba.

CHAPTER TWENTY-FIVE

Novelist Morris West wrote, "It costs so much to be a full human being that there are few who have the love and courage to pay the price. One has to abandon altogether the search for security and reach out to the risk of loving with both arms. One has to embrace life like a lover."

Although I don't feel that I embraced life like a lover or opened both arms to life, I feel like I might have performed these actions when I fell in love with the men in my life. I could not be half in love. It had to be all or nothing. I wish I could have been different when I was younger. It cost me a lot, but I had plenty of love and courage to pay the price over and over and over again. Like an idiot though, I kept picking the wrong men.

I also embraced my closet female friends with open arms. I am the kind of woman who is not afraid to say, "I love my girlfriends" and I will tell them I love them. I do, I did. Of course, there again as with the men but maybe not as much, those open arms meant exposing my heart and soul to pain, sadness and disappointment. It took many years to convince myself that maybe I expected too much. I never expected more than I could do or give, but then I guess I haven't known anyone quite like myself. I like to think like Anne Frank in that deep down everyone is good at heart. She said, "In spite of everything, I still believe that people are really good at heart."

A friend once said I was naïve about love and that, "You love like a child." I took it as a compliment. After all, isn't there something in the Bible to that effect?

Matthew 18:2-4 - *He called a little child to him, and placed the child among them. And he said: "Truly I tell you, unless you change and become like little children, you will never enter the kingdom of heaven.*

"You feel that you forgave your mother? "

I think so. I think I had to forgive her continually throughout my life. I must have. But after she passed away, I still felt like I had to forgive her. I remember telling my friend, Vinnie, that I hadn't forgiven her yet but was working on it. Vinnie said it might take some time but that was okay.

Maybe it is not so much of forgiveness that I had to do or have done, as much as I have had to accept her as she was and just go on, as well as everyone else that hurt me or performed unjust deeds to me or my daughter.

God has forgiven me of everything and we are to forgive each other.

Ephesians 4:32 - *Be kind and compassionate to one another, forgiving each other, just as in Christ God forgave you.* Here's another one I like or take seriously, Matthew 6:15 - *But if you do not forgive others their sins, your Father will not forgive your sins.*

I do have to say that God does forgive all of our sins. He does love us unconditionally and gives us new life. I believe that I did my time, hard time, when my mother was alive. I did the time in taking care of her and her children the best I could. I wasn't always nice and I sinned terribly both in my thoughts and actions, but in the end God forgave me. I truly believe His words and truly felt His forgiveness when He gave me a wonderful husband who truly loves me, when everything we attempted to do together just fell into place and when we haven't had any real stress or difficulties. We communicate very well with each other. I am finally free and forgiven. In a conversation with Alice (Reba's sister) she said "You were always forgiven, but when you met Kord it was all coming together for you."

My simple message: Forgive often. Accept yourself, God's love, forgiveness and only true love.

ABOUT THE AUTHOR

Georgianne Landy-Kordis studied screenwriting and directing at the University of Oklahoma. She has written, directed and produced promotional scripts as well as worked as a videographer through her own company, FIA/Films by Independent Artists, Inc. She is inspired to write human interest stories and offer emotional insight. She is happily married to Kenneth, loving their little Shih Tzu's and cattle ranching in Oklahoma. Her daughter is happily married and her teenage granddaughter is writing her first novel.

Made in the USA
Coppell, TX
27 January 2026

69166048R10128